Broadway and Wall Street: The History New York City's Most Famous Streets

By Charles River Editors

Promotion for *The Black Crook* (1866)

About Charles River Editors

Charles River Editors provides superior editing and original writing services across the digital publishing industry, with the expertise to create digital content for publishers across a vast range of subject matter. In addition to providing original digital content for third party publishers, we also republish civilization's greatest literary works, bringing them to new generations of readers via ebooks.

Sign up here to receive updates about free books as we publish them, and visit Our Kindle Author Page to browse today's free promotions and our most recently published Kindle titles.

Introduction

The Theater District of New York City

Broadway

"I would give the greatest sunset in the world for one sight of New York's skyline. The shapes and the thought that made them. The sky over New York and the will of man made visible... Let them come to New York, stand on the shore of the Hudson, look and kneel. When I see the city from my window - no, I don't feel how small I am - but I feel that if a war came to threaten this, I would like to throw myself into space, over the city, and protect these buildings with my body."
– Ayn Rand, *The Fountainhead*

Of all the great cities in the world, few personify their country like New York City. As America's largest city and best known immigration gateway into the country, NYC represents the beauty, diversity and sheer strength of the United States, a global financial center that has enticed people chasing the "American Dream" for centuries.

America's prototypical metropolis was once a serene landscape in which Native American tribes farmed and fished, but when European settlers arrived its location on the Eastern seaboard sparked a rapid transformation. Given its history of rapid change, it is ironic that the city's inhabitants often complain about the city's changing and yearn for things to stay the same. The website *EV Grieve*, whose name plays on the idea that the East Village "grieves" for the history and character the neighborhood loses every day to market forces and gentrification, regularly features a photo of some site, usually of little interest: an abandoned store, a small bodega, a vacant lot. The caption says, simply, that this is what the site looked like on a given day. The editors of the website are determined to document everything and anything for future generations.

That is hardly a modern phenomenon. New Yorkers have always grieved over the city's continuous upheavals and ever-increasing size and complexity. By the 1820s, Wall Street had lost whatever charm it might have had; former residents complained that two-story houses had given way to intimidating five-story office buildings. The *New York Commercial Advertiser* noted in 1825 that "Greenwich is no longer a country village," but rather an up-and-coming neighborhood. Today, it's hard to find a history of New York City that doesn't refer to Henry James's famous 1908 story *The Jolly Corner*, in which a man returns to New York after decades abroad only to be horrified by an unfamiliar hellscape of commercial growth. He finds his once-jolly childhood home nearly buried "among the dreadful multiplied numberings which seemed to him to reduce the whole place to some vast ledger-page, overgrown, fantastic, of ruled and criss-crossed lines and figures." The once-beloved city has transformed itself into "the mere gross generalisation of wealth and force and success." That childhood home—an 1830s townhouse—in fact belonged to the James family on Washington Square in Greenwich Village. It was destroyed to make way for New York University, which is today embroiled in yet another real estate saga as it plans to expand once again.

Broadway is more than just jazz hands, glittering costumes, tap numbers, and catchy show tunes that loop in one's mind for hours on end with the mildest provocation. Every year, thousands upon thousands of Broadway hopefuls climb on top of one another to hoist themselves onto the grand stage. Countless hours of training, coupled with blood, sweat, and tears, are poured into the craft, all for a chance to see their names emblazoned across the playbills and marquees – not to mention, perform for potential millions. Behind the dazzling lights and razzle and dazzle of Manhattan's legendary theater district is an equally colorful and riveting history. While hers is a story seasoned with innovative triumphs and remarkable firsts, it is also one plagued with scandal and controversy.

Broadway: The History and Legacy of New York City's Theater Center and Cultural Heart examines the history and legacy of the Big Apple's theater. Along with pictures of important people, places, and events, you will learn about Broadway like never before.

Wall Street Before Wall Street

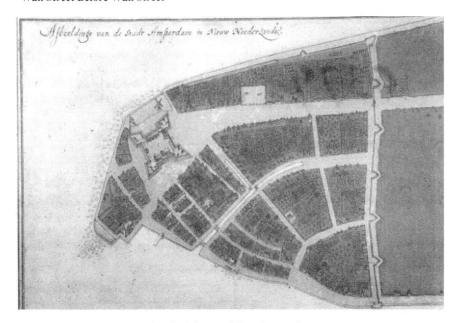

A colonial map of New Amsterdam

Wall Street has become a ubiquitous reference to the financial markets that call it home, but the name of the street itself provides a perfectly apt reference to its original use.

Manhattan has long been part of a bustling community, even before it formed the backbone of New York City. Centuries before New York City became a shining city of steel that enthralled millions of immigrants, Lenni-Lenape Indians, an Algonquin-speaking tribe whose name means "the People," lived in what would become New York, New Jersey, and Pennsylvania. They had lived there for at least 1,500 years and were mainly hunters and gatherers who would use well-worn paths that would one day bear the names of Flatbush Avenue, King's Highway, and Broadway.

The first known European sightings of the island and its inhabitants were made by the Italian explorer Giovanni da Verrazzano in 1524 and by the black Portuguese explorer Estaban Gomez in 1526. After the Englishman Henry Hudson, under the aegis of the Dutch East India Company, sailed by Manhattan in 1609, he returned home with good news and bad news. Like the other explorers before him, he hadn't been able to find a water route to the Orient. He had, however, returned with maps (confiscated by the British) and beaver pelts. With that, it became clear that the region around the bay that would take Hudson's name was a very promising new territory for trade and settlement, which would become a serious bone of contention between the Dutch and the British for the rest of the century.

In 1614, another East India merchant, Adriaen Block, entered through the narrows of the East River between Queens and Randall's Island, a difficult and dangerous passage that later sank numerous ships and that Block named Hell's Gate (Hellegat). The European world would know the name "Manhates" when Block returned to the Netherlands with new and improved maps. After that further exploration, the Dutch returned to build settlements on the southern tip of Manhattan and elsewhere, and by 1626 trade was brisk both between the Native Americans and the European settlers and between the settlers and their mother countries.

1626 was also the year that the famous "purchase" of Manhattan took place, a transaction for which no record has survived. Peter Minuit, the Director-General of New Amsterdam, paid out sixty guilders' worth of trade goods like cloth, kettles, tools, and wampum—an amount that's come down in history as being worth $24. While that sounds perversely low today, accountant types like to speculate with this amount, if the Lenni-Lenapes had invested it at a 10% interest rate over the centuries, it would today be worth $117 quadrillion—enough to buy present-day Manhattan many, many times over.

Many such purchases took place, but because Native Americans and Europeans had very different concepts of what it meant to "own" or "sell" land, misunderstandings—and violence— would frequently break out on both sides. Minor (and often unsubstantiated) thefts of property could ignite the colonists' wrath, resulting in such bloody skirmishes as the Pig War (1640) and the Peach Tree War (1655), named for the items allegedly stolen.

When the West India Company, which presided over Dutch trade in the Americas, was created in 1621, the little settlement at the tip of Manhattan began to both grow and falter. When Willem Kieft arrived as director in 1638, it was already a sort of den of iniquity, full of "mischief and perversity," where residents were given over to smoking and drinking grog and beer. Under Kieft's reign, more land was acquired mostly through bloody, all-but-exterminating wars with the Native American population, whose numbers also dwindled at the hands of European-borne diseases.

The Dutch tried to maintain good relations with all of the tribes for the sake of healthy trade but found themselves in the middle of conflicts among some of them, conflicts exacerbated by the fur trade. At Ft. Orange on the upper Hudson River, the powerful Mohawks of the Iroquois Confederacy challenged the Mahicans for access to the Dutch traders and attempted to become the middlemen with more inland tribes, so the Mahicans were forced to cede their land and relocate to the eastern side of the river.

In time, Indians who lived closer to New Amsterdam felt uncomfortable because the Dutch at

Ft. Orange had traded guns to their Mohawk enemies while they still had none to defend themselves. An additional factor causing Indians discomfort was the depletion of the fur-bearing animals with which they could trade for the commodities upon which they had become dependent.

As Dutch populations grew and expanded, the Indians became increasingly upset. By 1640, the Dutch had spread out from Manhattan and established new settlements on Staten Island, Long Island, and in the Bronx, which was named for Jonas Bronck after he settled there in 1639. They also settled in what is now Westchester County and New Jersey.

In September 1639, the relatively new director of the colony, Willem Kieft, set in motion a chain of events that led to warfare between the Dutch and some of the Lenni-Lenape around New Amsterdam when he demanded the Indians pay a tribute consisting of wampum, furs and corn. The 19th century historian, John Romeyn Brodhead, observed that this move on Kieft's part, which made sense from his point of view as a tax for services rendered by the Dutch to the Indians , understandably caused very strong ill feelings among the Indians. "They wondered how the sachem at the fort dared to exact such things from them.' 'He must be a very shabby fellow; he had come to live in their land when they had not invited him, and now came to deprive them of their corn for nothing.' They refused to pay the contribution, because the soldiers in Fort Amsterdam were no protection to the savages, who should not be called upon for their support; because they had allowed the Dutch to live peaceably in their country, and had never demanded recompense; because when the Hollanders, 'having lost a ship there, had built a new one, they had supplied them with victuals and all other necessaries, and had taken care of them for two winters, until the ship was finished,' and therefore the Dutch were under obligations to them; because they had paid full price for every thing they had purchased, and there was, therefore, no reason why they should supply the Hollanders now 'with maize for nothing;' and, finally, said the savages, because, 'if we have ceded to you the country you are living in, we yet remain masters of what we have retained for ourselves.'"

Kieft

Ultimately, warfare broke out in 1640. The Raritan band of the Lenni-Lenape were blamed for killing some pigs belonging to white settlers on Staten Island – white settlers typically let their swine run at large to forage in the woods -- although other evidence points to some servants of the Company as being the real culprits. Kieft decided that this was the right moment to show the Indians who was boss; he sent his secretary with a party of soldiers and sailors to demand reparations from the Indians and, if that were not forthcoming, to take as many of them as possible prisoner and destroy their corn fields. As a result, Dutch soldiers killed several Indians and took prisoner the brother of the sachem, and one of the soldiers on the boat back to Manhattan used a split piece of wood to torture the genitalia of the captured Indian.

In 1652, England and the Netherlands were at war, but heavy losses on both sides hurried the prospect of peace. Nevertheless, the two countries' representatives in the New World were increasingly hostile toward each other, even though they were an ocean away from the main belligerents. The Puritans of New England were said to be intent on attacking Manhattan, so preparations were made in New Amsterdam. A wall would be erected at New Amsterdam's northern border, at a cost of 5,000 guilders, with the labor being cheaply supplied by slaves. Made of 15 foot planks, bastions, cannons, and two gates (one at the corner of the present-day intersection of Wall St. and Pearl St., and the other at Wall St. and Broadway).

The Dutch referred to this stretch of road as "de Waal Straat," and it's believed that even before construction of that wall, there were earthen fortifications erected there to protect against Indian attacks. One early history claimed, "The red people from Manhattan Island crossed to the mainland, where a treaty was made with the Dutch, and the place was therefore called the Pipe of Peace, in their language, Hoboken. But soon after that, the Dutch governor, Kieft, sent his men out there one night and massacred the entire population. Few of them escaped, but they spread the story of what had been done, and this did much to antagonize all the remaining tribes against all the white settlers. Shortly after, Nieuw Amsterdam erected a double palisade for defense against its now enraged red neighbors, and this remained for some time the northern limit of the Dutch city. The space between the former walls is now called Wall Street, and its spirit is still that of a bulwark against the people."

The location of the wall would eventually become the center of the financial world, but ultimately, the wall proved as useless as all other Dutch defenses and strategies. In 1664, Colonel Richard Niccolls was sent by the English Duke of York to take Manhattan and all other Dutch holdings. Niccolls sent the Dutch colony's director, Peter Stuyvesant, a letter that promised life and liberty for all if the inhabitants would lay down their arms and surrender. Stuyvesant hid this letter and tore up another, but powerful residents in New Amsterdam forced him to give up in the face of too formidable an enemy. In the end, the diversity of New Amsterdam helped assure that the people would rather become part of New York City than lose everything. The Dutch briefly reclaimed the city, but the tide had turned, and New York became an English settlement. For their own part, the Lenni-Lenape who had lived there for so long dwindled until there were only about 200 of them left at the beginning of the 18th century.

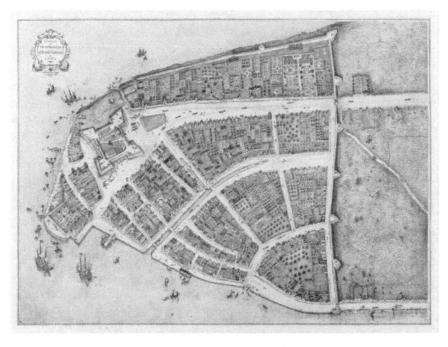

A map of New Amsterdam in 1660 with the wall on the far right of the settlement

Stuyvesant

Just before the end of the 17th century, the remainder of the actual wall on Wall Street was gone, and it would soon become a marketplace, which would make Wall Street a natural place for future exchanges.

The Birth of European Stock Exchanges

"After a certain point, money is meaningless. It ceases to become the goal. The game is what counts." – Aristotle Onassis, Greek shipping magnate

The idea of investment harks back to Ancient Greece. In a time when much of the world was uncharted and communities scattered around the world relied on ship tradesmen for resources, opportunity dawned. Ship captains reached out to the wealthy to finance their trading voyages, offering investors part of the profits from their loots. With massive but crudely built ships, equipment, and temperamental waters, this was considered one of the earliest practices of investment. Injecting money into these voyages was never a sure thing – the ships could come back with riches, or they were never to be seen again.

Ancient Romans were one of the first to sell stock for construction they could not finance on their own. These early stock brokers raked in plump profits from backing companies that built aqueducts, roads, and other public construction for the government. Across Europe, moneylenders became crucial to sealing the financial holes created by banks. These moneylenders began to barter debts between one another, some of which were government debts. Lenders hoping to relieve themselves of the burden of risky debts with ugly interest rates sought out debts they could handle from other lenders. As the practice went on, moneylenders began selling debt issues to customers. These customers became some of the earliest individual investors.

Come the 1300s, Venice became the forefront of the practice. Traveling merchants began to trade securities from various governments. These merchants were the first stock brokers. They roamed from door to door with slates clutched to their chests, which listed information on the different issues for sale.

In 1531, the world saw its first stock exchange in Antwerp, Belgium. Brokers and moneylenders alike congregated in the Antwerp Bourse, a grand and spacious wooden inn sporting high ceilings and a glass roof. Here, bonds, commodities, and promissory notes were dealt. Government, business, and individual debt issues would also be tackled. Though no actual stocks or shares existed in the 1500s, partnerships between businesses and financiers generated income much like stock does today.

Word of the goings-on in the Antwerp Bourse quickly spread. 40 years later, Queen Elizabeth I established The Royal Exchange in London, England. The architecture of the Antwerp Bourse largely inspired that of The Royal Exchange building.

When the 1600s rolled around, the Dutch, British, and French governments made a move that would pivot the course of economic history. All companies with "East India" in their name were granted charters. The imperialistic move ensured that profits were exclusive to seemingly everyone but the East Indies and Asian natives themselves.

During this time, sea voyages were still largely depended on for trade. Up to this point, investors were still backing one voyage at a time in faltering hopes of partial profits. These were known as the first limited liability companies. When the voyage ended, the company was scrapped, and a new company would be developed. Investors were coughing up currency for a wide range of voyages in one go. Needless to say, those who took the gamble on ships that never returned were faced with debilitating losses.

The merging of the East India companies meant the start of a new chapter. Instead of investing voyage by voyage, companies would have stocks that paid dividends on all voyages a single company undertook. Thus began the world's first joint stock companies.

With this in place, companies could construct larger and more powerful fleets, as well as reel in more profits from their shares. Investors were floating high on Cloud 9. Not only did these charters ban competition, the sheer size of these new companies meant a nifty payday for investors.

Shares were issued on paper, but there was no physical stock exchange for the East India companies. If an investor wanted to sell their share, they would have to employ a broker to carry out the task. Flyers with the latest debt issues and market shares were mailed as newsletters or posted on shop doors for public consumption.

More of the public became intrigued with investment and trade, with many in the middle class trying their hand at the game. But as they would soon learn, the game is a roller coaster of highs and lows, and it runs on unpredictable tracks. In the worst cases, a bubble slowly can slowly froth over an economy. A "bubble" is defined as rapid price increases triggered by a series of irrational market decisions. One inevitable prick could devastate the entire economy of a community.

The earliest record of an economic bubble took place in the Netherlands in 1637 – Tulip Mania. Many have since studied this infamous incident as a 400-year-old cautionary tale, one that Gordon Gekko himself has framed in his office. In the early 1600s, tulips were all the rage in the Netherlands. The Dutch fell smitten with the pretty pastel flowers, and it soon became a must-have in all households, the hottest commodity on the market. The rarity of these seasonal flowers only spurred the demand. People started pressuring the suppliers for reassurance that they would have their beloved tulips by the end of the year. To remedy the demand, suppliers set up a "future's market." In simpler terms, they began taking pre-orders. During the off-season, suppliers sold customers IOUs for tulips, which they could exchange for tulips when they were available.

It wasn't long before suppliers took notice of the unbelievable demand and began jacking up the prices. By 1637, the ludicrously inflated prices took its toll, and the Dutch found themselves in piping-hot water. The price of a perishable bulb was valued at 10 times the yearly salary of a skilled craftsman. To put this into perspective, this meant 10 years of hard labor to get one's hands on a measly flower, only for it to shrivel in 10 days or less. The bubble was eventually popped, and prices plummeted to reasonable levels. Unfortunately, a large number of families were unable to escape from the tulip contracts they had signed at the peak of Tulip Mania, and as a result, lost their family fortunes.

Another significant historical bubble came into play in England, most commonly known as the South Sea Bubble of 1720. The British East India Company was operating on a legal monopoly. This meant an independent company owned all or the majority of a particular market with the government's approval. With little to no competition, investors soon had dollar signs for eyes. Others began wising up to the fortunes being made by investors when they sold their shares, and wanted in. But with the economical boom growing more explosive by the minute, issuing shares was going unregulated. Things quickly got out of hand.

Robert Harley and John Blunt, the founders of the South Sea Company, were also granted a similar charter by King George I. The SSC began passing out countless re-issues of shares like candy, most of which sold as soon as they were listed. Before the first company ship even budged, the SSC used the excessive riches they made from the eager investors to set up state-of-the-art offices in the swankiest parts of the city.

Devious businessmen soon caught on to the SSC's success. Seeing that the SSC had done nothing but sell shares before they even started their first venture, crooked businessmen emerged from the shadows. They approached the public with brand new shares from completely fabricated companies.

Surprisingly, investors were duped by these fictitious ventures and the shady broker's fraudulent claims. In an effort to boost capital and stock prices, these claims became creatively absurd. This included proposals for hair trading and reclaiming sunshine from plants and vegetables. Some invested in wild inventions such as a wheel for perpetual motion and a new-age device that would convert chickens into sheep. One bold company sold shares for a mysterious product so important and shrouded in secrecy, the investors themselves weren't allowed to know what it was. This proved to be a fruitful tactic as the company shares promptly sold out.

Their method of salesmanship was so toxic, a term was coined for it – blind pools. Blind pools are stock offerings with muddy to no investment goals. Investors relied on the name of the individual or company. These risky offerings come with paltry restrictions that are often left unguarded.

Harsh reality struck when the SSC was unable to pay any dividends from their nearly non-existent profits. The crash that ensued crippled the British economy, causing the government to banish the issuing of shares. This ban wouldn't be lifted until 1825.

Soon, the reputations of stock brokers soured. Those on the sidelines agreed that the greedy and dishonest individuals, some of which were disgraced government officials, got what was coming to them. The public disdain for stock brokers soon spread around the globe. It did not help matters when escaped Scottish murderer, John Law, trapped the French public in his blind pools, promising them shares in imaginary gold mines.

A History of Theater

"All the world's a stage, and all the men and women merely players: they have their exits and their entrances; and one man in his time plays many parts." – Jacques, "As You Like It" by William Shakespeare

Dazzling light bulb studded signs, shimmering costumes, fantastic flurries of feathers, moving monologues, and colorful choreography woven into magnificent musical numbers. Bouquets and single-stemmed roses tossed onto the stage at curtain call as the audience rises in unison, their hands joining together in spirited applause. Seeing as this is what usually springs to one's mind when one daydreams about the theatre, it is no mystery why millions are drawn to Broadway. It is the epitome of razzmatazz and surrealism, where theatrical souls vie for the grandest and brightest of spotlights. It is where audiences drift away from the real world, where they can lose themselves in the splendors of the stage for a few precious hours.

The art of drama has existed for thousands of years. As early as the 6th century BCE, the followers of Dionysus, a Greek god of wine and fertility, incorporated the primitive craft into their rituals. The cult ceremonies held by these followers are what many would now deem bizarre, for they involved devotees wielding phallic symbols, ripping apart tethered animals, and wolfing down the remnants. The same archaic festivities saw its women dancing violently until rendered hysterical. In time, these ceremonies were tamed with structure. Followers developed choirs that transformed Greek myths into songs with simple, often monotone melodies.

Later on, a priest by the name of Thespis revolutionized the art by seasoning the choral songs with dialogue. Thespis is therefore considered one of – if not the – first actors of the world, and is why both aspiring and accomplished actors today continue to brand themselves "Thespians." His work was so revered in his time that upon joining a competition for tragedies in Athens, he took home the trophy for first prize. From then on, these contests were held annually in the city of Dionysia. 4 of the most acclaimed playwrights in Greece penned 3 tragedies and 1 satire, their works performed on a makeshift wooden stage furnished with false greenery.

The blossoming culture of theatre was not merely restricted to the West. One of the most fascinating types of traditional Japanese theatre is kabuki. This unique style of dance-drama, though known for its all-male ensembles, was sparked by Izumo no Okuni and her all-women dance troupes. They were regarded as so risque that kabuki performances by females were banned by the Shogun in 1629, which in effect, opened the door to male kabuki actors, who then dominated the scene. Another in the dance-drama genre was the noh, recognizable by its use of wooden masks crafted in a wide range of designs to display a variety of symbolic facial expressions. These masks were not only difficult to duplicate, they could be interpreted in different ways depending on the angle of one's view.

China was another major player in Eastern theatre. During the Shang Dynasty, which lasted between 1600 to 1046 BCE, the hunting dances of their ancestors were updated with "animal movements." The Zhou Dynasty set the stage for the first chorus dances – the wu, strictly performed by the men, and xi, by women. Comedies that employed "dwarfs," clowns, and acrobats were another hit with Chinese audiences. Early Chinese plays were usually composed of equal parts choruses and mime.

The theatre was a crucial element of the culture, so much so that baixi, or in English, "a hundred entertainments," was established by the court. Once or twice a year, the public gathered at these festivals, where they enjoyed an elaborate variety show brought to life by its glittering cast of martial arts masters, acrobats, musicians, dancers, jugglers, and circus acts. Beautiful maidens with immaculately painted faces danced emotively with their arms, their cascading sleeves of silk, known as "water sleeves," fluttering daintily as they moved.

British theatre was said to have spawned from religious storytelling during medieval times. Entertainment was desperately needed to divert the public's attention from the turmoil within the Church, as well as the merciless outbreaks of the Black Death. The "storytelling" was classed in 2 categories – mystery cycles, which brought biblical stories to the stage, and miracle plays, dramas that revolved around the lives of saints. As it was the local parishes that mobilized these plays, a moral lesson was embedded into these stories.

The English city of York soon emerged as one of the frontrunners when it came to mystery cycles. Every year, on the Feast of Corpus Christi, the streets were awakened at 4 in the morning with a parade through the streets. Banners led to staged performances by actors posted at 12 different locations scattered throughout the city, each presenting a pivotal piece of Christian history.

Seating on wooden scaffolding served as bleachers of sorts for the royalty and nobility who wished to spectate. At least 48 different plays were carried out in a single day. Rather than parishes, York play companies were operated by different guilds. Shipwrights, for example, were placed in charge of demonstrating the building of Noah's Ark, whereas the famous water-to-wine scene at the Wedding of Cana was performed by winemakers.

It was during the reign of King Henry VIII, the monarch who created the Church of England in 1534, that religious plays were blacklisted to put a damper on the spreading of the Catholic message. The trend began to pick up throughout the mid-16th century, and came into full swing during the Elizabethan Era. In 1576, the first modern playhouse was erected in northern London by James Burbage, a friend of the then up-and-coming playwright, William Shakespeare. The playhouse, dubbed "The Theatre," was a great 3-story structure fashioned out of timber that encircled a wide and elevated stage, complete with a pair of staircases on either side for easy access to the upper galleries. A great many acting troupes would grace this stage, but it was Shakespeare's company, the Chamberlain's Men, that thousands flocked to see.

A 17ᵗʰ century depiction of the Globe Theatre

Like the kabuki stage, the acting profession in Shakespeare's day boxed women out of the equation, a tradition that remained unchanged until King Charles II was crowned monarch in 1660. As interest in the theatrical arts continued to swell, more acting companies banded together, while others expanded their operations. The most prominent companies developed hierarchical systems of their own.

Actors who owned shares in the companies were aptly named "sharers," and thus earned their portion of the profits. Hirelings worked part-time and were compensated with weekly wages. Actors who took on menial or female roles, known as "apprentices," were placed in the bottom of the pyramid, and while some worked full hours, apprentices were given the lowest salaries. The average company churned out and performed anywhere between 30 to 40 plays each year, a figure that steadily increased in the ensuing years to keep up with the demand.

Enter the early days of Colonial America in the early 17ᵗʰ century, where entertainment was limited to unsophisticated parlor games and handcrafted amusements. According to John Smith, to balance out the strife and maintain one's sanity during the first years of colonization, only 4 hours were spent at work, and the rest devoted to "pastimes and merry exercise." One of the most common mediums of colonial entertainment was music. Brass cymbals, jaw harps, tambourines, trumpets, and other musical contraptions were used to liven up the chilly and often grim interiors of homes and public spaces, as well as to signal ships and military exercises.

Toy houses, windmills, and other elaborate miniatures whittled out of wood and carved out of copper and other metals were uncovered at the excavation site of James Fort, which gave evidence to one of the ways soldiers entertained themselves. While these pint-sized recreations sufficed for some, most quenched their thirst for entertainment with an array of gambling games. More than 60 gaming dice made from ivory, bone, and lead were found in the same fort alone. The sovereigns back home decreed that anyone caught in dice or card games, such as "put" (an early version of poker), would be sentenced to the dreaded "Gallies" for up to a year, but this did little to discourage their popularity with the soldiers. Chess, which eventually caught on with the upper classes, was another game detested by King James I, who condemned it as an evil that "filleth and troubleth men's heads."

Leisure in colonial households usually consisted of storytelling and cheap parlor games. One of these games, "Question and Answer," was a precursor to the modern day "Truth or Dare." Family members scribbled questions of outlandish to dark natures onto separate cards, which were then shuffled, and later drawn and answered by each player. The sale of board games became a profession of its own, with its salesmen peddling games such as the "Royal and Most Pleasant Game of the Goose," which was a flat board with a circular track, and tiny tokens that moved forward to the roll of the dice. Billiard tables and backgammon boards later became some of the wealthy people's favorite avenues of entertainment.

As was the norm at the time, recreational activities were enjoyed mostly by men, while women stayed home to tick off household chores while looking after the children. When women did manage to scrounge up the time for themselves, they knitted, played indoor games, and took up other extracurricular pursuits at home, for they were banned from entering local clubs or taverns. Apart from tabletop games, men tickled their fancies with cockfights, boxing, tomahawk throwing, and shooting games, such as the sport of dueling.

By the turn of the 18th century, the population of the colonies had ballooned to approximately 650,000 residents. Massachusetts was home to somewhere between 70 to 80,000; Virginia in second place at 60,000, half of them slaves; and in New York, 30,000. The thriving colonies continued to beat its wings with promising vigor, its strength powered by the booming tobacco and sugar industries. Colonies in North Carolina found their footing as manufacturing centers pumped out ample supplies of turpentine, white pine ship masts, and hemp rope. The escalation in slavery, however controversial, built the pedestal for a wealthy colonial class called the "gentry."

The rise of the new class amplified the demand for more vehicles of entertainment, which segued into a new chapter of Colonial American culture. While records have survived of American plays dating as far back as 1665, sprouts only began to surface from the stirring seeds in the increasingly prosperous climate of the 1700s. A contract for the construction of the first American playhouse, unveiled to the public as the "Play Booth Theatre," was signed on July 11, 1716, by a merchant and dance troupe manager named William Levingston.

Levingston purchased a lot about 3 ½ acres in size on the Palace Green, which he kitted out with a dwelling space, stable, kitchen, bowling alley, and a playhouse. The open-air playhouse, a moderately decorated 2-story structure about 86.5 feet long and 30 feet wide, would become host to the Williamsburg Company of Comedians. On May 28, 1718, the birthday of King George I, the Play Booth Theatre rolled out its first play, one put together and financed by Governor Alexander Spotswood.

Spotswood

Attached to the contract were teachers from Levingston's former dancing school in New Kent County, Charles and Mary Stagg, bound to the agreement as "indentured partners." As per the terms of the contract, the Staggs served as actors and dance teachers, instructing musicians, dancers, and actors Levingston promised to ship over from the motherland. The Staggs received salaries, but were made to cough up percentages of their earnings to Levingston over the next 3 years. Fortunately for the Staggs, they enjoyed a fairly lucrative career for the next 2 decades, capitalizing on Virginia's newfound love for dancing. Those who had chanced upon some money hoped to echo the lifestyles of the elite back home, and began to organize formal dance parties in private estates, taverns, and later, clubs and halls built precisely for this purpose.

By the 1730s, the reins to the theatre and its buildings had been transferred to Dr. George Gilmer, Sr., who owned a successful apothecary around the bend of the lot. For a time, it was used as a space for amateur dramas such as The Recruiting Officer and The Tragedy of Cato, the second written by English playwright, Joseph Addison, about the legendary Stoic figure that squirmed free from Caesar's suffocating fist. Following Gilmer's promotion to mayor in 1746, the Play Booth was dismantled and replaced with a new courthouse.

Though it appeared as if the flames of the new colonial art had begun to flicker in Virginia, their neighbors up north were determined to keep that fire burning with a blaze brighter than anyone had ever seen before.

Broadway Beginnings

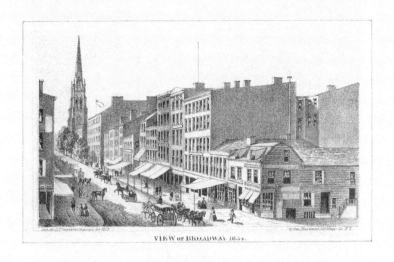

1834 depiction of Broadway

Broadway in the 1860s

"I regard the theatre as the greatest of all art forms, the most immediate way in which a human being can share with another the sense of what it is to be a human being." – attributed to Oscar Wilde

Broadway is thought to be one of New York's oldest thoroughfares. Centuries before the complex of theatres arose, it was a winding, undisturbed path known as the "Wickquasgeck Trail," populated by rich collections of poplar, chestnut, and pine trees, and spacious stretches of strawberry fields. This route had been established by the Lenape Indians as a way to cut through the swampy and rocky terrains of Manhattan Island.

The Colony of New Amsterdam, the capital of the Dutch-owned New Netherland, was then captured peacefully by an English squadron led by Colonel Richard Nicolls in 1664. Shortly after, New Amsterdam was renamed "New York" as a tribute to the Duke of York, who would later become England's King James II. Several Dutch regions, properties, and streets were maintained but Anglicized with new names. Breuckelen was rechristened as "Brooklyn," and Harleem shortened to "Harlem." North-south portions of the Wickquasgeck Trail appropriated by the Dutch, which they named "Breede Wegh," was reintroduced as "Broadway."

As the previous Dutch settlers were devout Protestants that showed little to no interest in the dramatic arts, it would take another century before the New Yorkers warmed up to the concept. Up until the 1700s, settlers relied on the magic of booze not to just speed up the hands of time, it had become a crucial component of everyday life at a time when pure drinking water was a rarity. It was believed that alcoholic beverages could stimulate the weak, heal the ailing, and supposedly possessed anti-aging properties.

As a result, settlers from all classes and ages kicked off their days with a refreshing tonic and ended the day with a hefty nightcap. Booze became a must-have at all social events, from weddings and funerals to election day parties. Craftsmen, merchants, and even school teachers were known to tip back their jugs at work to keep them "energized" throughout the day. Shoppers were seen marking off their shopping lists with bottles and flasks in hand. Towards the late 18th century, the average American over the age of 15 was consuming approximately 34 gallons of beer and cider, 5 gallons of rum, whiskey, and other distilled spirits, and at least a gallon of wine. The New Yorkers added to the breweries set up by the Dutch settlers in New Amsterdam, which supplied the taverns and ordinaries cropping up around the region in droves.

That said, there were those who voiced their concerns about the harmful effects of the colonists' heavy drinking habits. In 1622, the Virginia Company of London wrote a letter to Jamestown's Governor Francis Wyatt addressing this very sentiment. James Oglethorpe, an ex-member of Parliament and the founder of Georgia, was another that attempted to drain the booze barrels of his utopian colony by placing restrictions on rum, as well as slavery and land ownership. Benjamin Franklin, who was known to have been something of a beer enthusiast himself, promoted moderation in drinking in his writings, and once declared that "nothing is more like a fool than a drunken man."

In an effort to curtail their unbridled boozing, colonists found alternatives in tea and coffee, which soon became household staples in New York. Enterprising minds opted out of the overcrowded tavern industry and set out to kindle and thereby profit from the settlers' nostalgia by building London-style coffeehouses across the American colonies. Here, families and friends gathered for piping-hot mugs of dark-brown, caffeinated goodness, the aromatic scent of boiling coffee grounds wafting across the enclosed space.

At times, these coffeehouses, particularly the establishments in New York, served as governmental and public forums. The earliest mention of a coffee house in said colony is the King's Arms in Broadway, its construction commissioned by one John Hutchins in 1696. The King's Arms, which sat by the Trinity Church, was a 2-story wooden cottage with a facade made of pale yellow bricks transported all the way from Holland.

Sitting on its roof was an observatory with a handful of seats that overlooked a spectacular view of the sparkling bay and bustling city. The main room on the ground floor was furnished with booths veiled with emerald-green curtains, its privacy perfect for romantic drinks and private transactions. Rooms on the second floor were closed off to the public and reserved for merchants, magistrates, and local leaders to conduct their businesses.

Another part of the second floor was sectioned off to quarter guests who wished to lodge in the inn. Given the orderly, professional atmosphere of coffeehouses, these establishments were most frequented by merchants and white-collar patrons, whereas taverns attracted drunkards and unfamiliar town-hoppers. On top of council meetings and general assemblies, the King's Arms was said to have held their own version of open mic nights, staging some of the first amateur theatrical performances of Manhattan.

In February of 1750, a Philadelphian company of comedians known as the Murray-Kean Company, arrived in New York. Little is known about the company's founders, Walter Murray and Thomas Kean, apart from the fact that they were English-born actors and managers who had recently wrapped up a tour in Barbados, Jamaica, and other destinations in the West Indies. Some speculate that they may have been trained by John Moody, a seasoned barber-turned-actor who hailed from London's fabled Drury Lane.

Moody started out as a comedian, carving out a name for himself with his strong diction and hearty Irish brogue. Now that he had his foot through the door, Moody did not want to be pigeonholed as a comedian when it was tragedy where his heart lay, so he approached his managers and requested new roles that reflected his true passion. When he was rebuffed, Moody, refusing to be typecasted, resigned, boarded a ship, and set sail for Jamaica, touching ground in 1745. There, he set up his own acting troupe and recruited actors from London to his fledgling company, which was presumably how Murray and Kean entered the picture.

Murray and Kean appealed to Governor George Clinton for a license that permitted them to act in the colony. The pair brought with them a proposal outlining the property they had set their eyes on – a building on Nassau Street by the junction of Pearl Street and Maiden Lane, one previously belonging to the deceased Honorable Rip Van Dam. Once all renovations were completed on March of 1750, what was now the New Theatre, or the Nassau Street Theatre, opened its doors and courteously welcomed the public.

Clinton

An early 19ᵗʰ century depiction of the New Theatre

That day, the first formal theatre in New York treated the public to a splendid viewing of Shakespeare's highly-acclaimed Richard III. Among the cast were Dicky Murray, Walter's son, as well as Nancy George and a Madame Osborne, the latter duo billed as "chief ladies in comedy and tragedy." In December of that year, they made history once more when they performed John Gay's The Beggar's Opera, the first documented musical in New York. The gritty satirical tale was both applauded and scorned, for the story was centered upon a gangmaster and his thief of a son-in-law, and colored with bandits, prostitutes, pimps, and other racy characters from London's underbelly.

The theatre awed anyone who laid eyes on it. The handsome building with tall gabled roofs, though only 2 floors, could cater to up to 280 people at once. A sleek wooden stage standing 5 feet off the ground sat in its core, which was outfitted with a velvety dark-green curtain, half a dozen "wax lights" in front of the stage, and an extra chandelier adorned with multiple candles for added lighting. Paper screens were set up on either side which acted as wings, where actors could enter and exit the stage; it was also where the backdrops were stowed. The plays were to be accompanied by live music, provided by the small orchestra, consisting of a German horn, flute, and drum set, by the foot of the stage. The first plays made use of 2 full-sized backdrops – one a mighty stone castle, and the other, a vibrantly painted mountainous landscape with a twisting river.

Instead of the plush, cushiony theatre seats of today, the audience back then made do with rickety wooden benches. In a time before indoor heating, audience members had to take turns huddling around a large stove near the entrance, so many elected to bring their own "charcoal foot warmers" from home. All the props and amenities were made easily-collapsible so they could be rapidly put together and efficiently taken apart. This was common business practice with theatres of the time, which was why constructing such establishments cost only a sliver of what one would cost today. To put this into perspective, the Beekman Street Theatre, the fourth theatre to be opened in New York, cost the investors no more than $1,625 (roughly $48,750 USD today) from start to finish.

For the next 2 seasons, which typically consisted of 39 weeks, the Murray-Kean Company worked around the clock to ensure that their performances, which were scheduled twice a week, ran swimmingly each time. Included in their lengthy repertoire was Thomas Otway's tragedy, Orphan; George Farquhar's The Recruiting Officer, a campy comedy about an "odd couple" of officers; and farces such as Henry Fielding's comic opera, The Mock Doctor; and David Garrick's Miss in Her Teens. These performances began with a swell of the opening music provided by the in-house orchestra, followed by the prologue, main piece, epilogue, solo dances, then an afterpiece, and closed with specialty acts, which was usually a group jig performed by the entire cast to end the night with a bang.

Alas, on June 17, 1751, the founders, longing for the road, made the collective decision to heed their restless feet and shut the doors of the theatre. The company relocated to Williamsburg, where they stayed for some time before touring across Maryland. There, they presented their acts in the backs of warehouses, courthouses, and other spare rooms of both functioning and defunct establishments.

Noting the success of the Murray-Kean Company in New York, other theatre and dance companies gradually followed suit. These so-called "stock theatre companies" would be modeled after the "star system" of Great Britain. In the hopes of both maintaining and boosting attendance rates, a special guest star would be featured for either one or a set number of shows. These guest stars were freelance actors who had paved a field of profession of their own, earning their living by roaming across the country for these one-off gigs.

In these stock theatre companies, an actor-manager captained the ship, supervising and signing off on all matters relating to business and production. They, too, held the power to tweak or rewrite scenes from a playwright's work if they so wished, a practice that persisted until the Dramatic Copyright Act of 1833, which forbade managers from making any alterations on "printed plays."

The Murray-Kean Company, which initially implemented the star system, was one of the first to spot and mold what became known as the "combination system." It no longer made sense to employ costly guest stars when they could be pocketing potentially twice the profits without them if they took their act on the road. And so, the company did just that.

The American Revolutionary War, which had been precipitated by the fiercely boiling tensions between British authorities and the colonists, was already over a year old by June of 1776. The colonists, aggravated by what they construed as unjust taxation, were insistent on breaking free from the shackles of the British Empire. The Continental Congress, a convention of delegates, was assembled to govern the Thirteen Colonies on their road to independence.

When the First Continental Congress convened 2 years earlier, those present made the firm decision to cut all trade with Britain, which was only to be lifted if the opposing party agreed to their conditions, their freedom ranking at the top of the list. Furthermore, an excerpt from Article 8 read, "And we will discountenance (object to) and discourage every species of extravagance and dissipation, especially all horse-racing, all kinds of gaming, cockfighting, exhibitions of shows, plays, and other expensive diversions and entertainments..." Shortly after the proclamation went into effect, theatre companies were left with no choice but to desert their playhouses and seek other business ventures elsewhere, mostly overseas. And with that, the growth of the theatre industry in the colonies grinded to a halt.

Unsurprisingly, the outlawing of theatre did not sit well with those who regarded it as their bread and butter; one critic, British Major General John Burgoyne, poetically groaned, "In Britain once...Freedom was vital struck by party rage...Then sunk the stage, quelled by the Bigot

Roar, Truth fled with Sense, and Shakespeare charmed no more...Say then, ye Boston prudes...is this a task unworthy of the Fair?...Perish the narrow thought, the slanderous tongue, where the heart's right, the action can't be wrong."

Burgoyne

Revival

"Stay – not now, it will be noted; when the procession moves, then steal away by the upper path." – spoken by Wolfenstein in "The Black Crook"

Despite the congressional nationwide ban on theatre, the love for the craft could not be extinguished. British soldiers stationed in the colonies took it upon themselves to form their own military theatrical companies, as seen in the organizations headed by General William Howe, based in Philadelphia; General Henry Clinton in New York; and the previously mentioned General John Burgoyne in Boston. Some soldiers, such as Major John André, did not belong to any set guild, but instead, flitted from one base to another to perform, act as stagehands, or complete whatever task was assigned to them. The artistically blessed André was said to have been so dedicated to the art that he forwent his soldierly duties and spent his stint in Philadelphia painting a gorgeous and intricately detailed backdrop to be used in the Southwark Theatre.

Many of these military men, such as Burgoyne, seized the opportunity to use these performances – at this time, an especially coveted form of entertainment – as a platform to push their political agendas. In Boston, Burgoyne wrote a farce entitled The Boston Blockade, laced with pro-Britain commentary and his frustrations with his American rivals. George Washington, one of the primary antagonists of this play, was portrayed as an ungainly and "uncouth figure," who sported a loose, unflattering wig, moved with an "awkward gait," and lugged around a discolored sword. Included in his lyrics was a clear-cut threat to the "Tyrants":

"Ye...yantkied Prigs,

Who are Tyrants in Custom,

Yet call yourselves Whigs,

In return for the favors you've lavished on me,

May I see you all hanged upon Liberty Tree."

Meanwhile, in New York, Clinton's military company opted to avoid the propaganda route. They resumed the colony's Shakespearean tradition, and enacted 6 of the celebrated wordsmith's bestselling works – 5 dramas and 1 comedy. While a company in New York had yet to compose their own original plays, it was at this time that they began to experiment with their own prologues.

When the American Revolutionary War drew to a close in 1783, cementing the colonies' newfound independence, the companies who had fled made their slow return to the theatrical scenes across the 13 states. The John Street Theatre, the 5th theatre built in New York, was said to have been the only theatre to survive the war, as it had been used and maintained by one of General Clinton's companies. Construction of the theatre, which was founded by the Hallams, a family of theatrical bigwigs in Virginia, was directed by English actor-manager, David Douglass. At its prime, the theatre could entertain up to an estimated 500 guests at a time, equipped with a broad center stage highlighted by the glow radiating from the oil lamp chandeliers hovering from above.

A depiction of the interior of the John Street Theatre

Unfortunately, Douglass' designs, particularly its unappealing rusty-red wooden facade and aging interior, could not survive the fast-paced resurgence of theatre following the war, and began to wind down sometime in the late 1790s. By 1795, the company decided to retire the dilapidated, pitiful excuse of a theatre, and began to map out plans for a brand-new establishment in Manhattan's Park Row. 3 years later, after its brief service as a storage house for hay and fodder, the John Street Theatre was stripped bare and permanently laid to rest.

On January 29, 1798, the Park Theatre unfurled its welcome mat to the public, treading familiar ground with its first play – Shakespeare's As You Like It. The new playhouse did not disappoint, delivering every drop of the grandeur its architects had promised. Standing on Park Row's Chatham Street was a lordly 3-story building of stone, fitted with matching arched windows on the lower floors, and a set of square windows on the topmost floor. The theatre boasted 2,000 seats, its tickets swiftly vanishing at 50 cents a head.

A depiction of the interior of the Park Theatre

Come the mid-1820s, the affluent families residing in the Bowery neighborhood of what is now the Lower East Side of Manhattan had begun to grow envious of the Park Theatre's success. The opening of Lafayette Street, which ran parallel to the Bowery, elevated the wealthy neighborhood's already attractive property values. In a move to class up the Bowery to a level that surpassed, or at the very least, matched Park Row's, the richest families of the neighborhood collaborated to build a theatre of their own – one that would put the prestigious Park Theatre to shame.

Among its most noteworthy investors was James Hamilton, son of Alexander Hamilton, and Samuel Gouverneur, the son-in-law of the United States' fifth president, James Monroe. The Bowery Theatre, otherwise known by its alternative moniker, The New York Theatre, announced its opening in late October of 1826. Going against the Shakespearean tradition, the Bowery troupe had Thomas Holcroft's comedy, The Road to Ruin, rehearsed to a tee.

Upon the completion of the theatre, its designer, Connecticut-born architect Ithiel Town, gazed upon his creation, exuding with pride. The investors, equally pleased, patted him on the back, for they had undoubtedly triumphed in their mission to outshine its rival in Park Row. The Bowery Theatre's architecture was flavored with Neoclassical elements, particularly its distinctive Corinthian pillars and accordingly ornamented interior. More importantly, it broke new records with its seating capacity of 3,000. Frances Trollope, a 19th century novelist, had this to remark about the Bowery: "...It is indeed as pretty a theatre as I ever entered, perfect as to size and proportion, elegantly decorated, and the scenery and machinery equal to any in London."

When the manager, Thomas Hamblin, received full control of the playhouse in September of 1830, the Bowery Theatre revised its business model. To further set it apart from the Park

Theatre, which selected works that underscored "European high culture," the plays at the Bowery became a soapbox for the average man, emphasizing on the problems of the "ordinary" in society, as well as Pro-American ideals. Hamblin also substituted kerosene lamps and candles with gas-powered lighting. Even more impressive, Hamblin tested out and constantly improvised special effects techniques with water and fire.

At first, those at Park Row scoffed at the modified billing of the Bowery, which now lined up performances that targeted the working class, such as animal acts, melodramas, and black-face minstrel shows. Its crude audience soon earned the theatre a new nickname – the Slaughterhouse. But when the streak of sold out tickets at the Bowery remained unbroken for quite some time, those at Park Theatre were forced to bite their tongues.

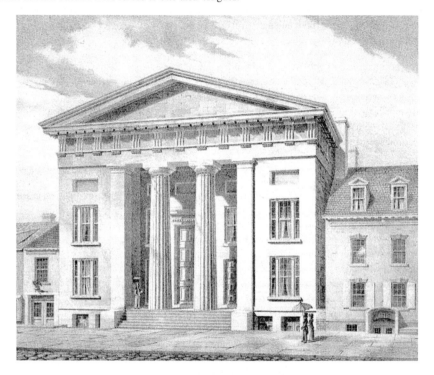

The Bowery Theatre

One of the first playhouses built on Broadway was Niblo's Garden on Prince Street in 1834. Prior to its conversion to a theatre, it was a resort owned by William Niblo, a coffeehouse mogul and former caterer. The getaway came with a refreshment station that served ice cream, lemonade, coffee, and other beverages, as well as an opulent garden, guarded by white board fences, that spanned an entire block surrounded by the streets of Prince, Broadway, Houston, and Crosby. Smack dab in the middle of the resort lived an unroofed courtyard where visitors socialized with drinks and open-air concerts. The courtyard was especially heavenly at night, for it was kissed with the light from the hundreds of multicolored glass lanterns strung up around the space. To keep out the "trouble," entry to the garden was priced at 50 cents a piece.

It was in 1834 that Niblo decided to upgrade his beloved garden with a Grand Saloon, the first of its concert halls, which played various musical genres; he then dabbled in the art of Vaudeville. When the theatre was engulfed by the flames of a wayward fire in mid-September of 1846, its architects worked to perfect a fortified model that would dwarf the last. 3 years later, an enormous theatre with a maximum capacity of 3,200 guests stood in its place, one that bore the latest, top-of-the-line facilities and theatrical equipment. Niblo's theatre reoriented towards Italian opera, so admission prices hiked up to $2 each.

The prices turned off only an insignificant fraction of the audience, for the one-of-a-kind and star-studded acts at Niblo's Garden repeatedly filled every last seat of the theatre. Among the attendees were the loyal fans of Bennett Barrow, Maggie Mitchell, and E.L. Davenport. Tickets were particularly difficult to snag in 1855, when renowned French acrobat and tightrope-walker, Charles Blondin, was booked at the garden. Towards the 1860s, the garden, keeping up with the times, dipped its toes in comedy.

In 1866, The Black Crook, a masterpiece by American playwright, Charles M. Barras, made its debut on the Garden stage. This was said to have been the earliest known "book musical" melodrama, which planted the foundations of Broadway's legacy. The fresh genre, which was told in songs, medleys, and sometimes, spoken dialogue, was distinctive for its "serious" and organized plot lines, as well as its attention to character development.

William Wheatley, the manager of the Garden, was eager to make a spectacle of the first modern day Broadway musical. To accomplish this, he hired artists to create multiple backdrops, extra stagehands, and cast over a hundred ravishing female dancers. The musical was witnessed by Mark Twain himself, who fondly recounted the performance. "The scenery and legs are everything..." he gushed, "Girls – nothing but a wilderness of girls – stacked up, pile on pile, away aloft to the dome of the theatre...dressed with a meagerness that would make a parasol blush." The Black Crook ran for about 16 months, and in that short time, grossed over a million dollars, a figure unheard of back in the day.

It appeared that every theatrical investor at this point was looking to one up the other. On November 22, 1847, the Astor Place Opera House, a concept birthed by Edward Fry, the brother of the symphonic composer, William Henry Fry, came into fruition. As instructed by Fry, its designer, Isaiah Rogers, who specialized in the Greek Revival style, built a luxurious playhouse fit for only the top tiers of society.

In place of stiff wooden benches were individual upholstered seats, as well as 2 projecting balconies that provided a first-class view of the stage. The best seats in the house, including the balconies, had to be reserved several weeks, sometimes even months, in advance. Only 500 seats, which were placed furthest away from the stage on an isolated loft of its own, were made available to the "general public." To top it all off, a strict dress code was enforced upon the guests. One had to be dressed in their finest suits and evening gowns, sport clean-shaven and fully made up faces, and accessorize with gloves and jewelry.

Astor Place authorities were under the impression that staving off the rowdy working class, a culture derogatorily referred to as the "Bowery Boys," would keep the fracas often associated with these people at bay. Only, the snobbery did anything but sit well with the Bowery Boys, who yearned for their fair share of the forbidden fruit. On the evening of March 7, 1849, during a performance of Macbeth, dozens of the working class in intentionally inappropriate attire filed into the opera house and plopped down on the theatre's premium seats.

Their arrival sent a shudder down the spines of Astor authorities, who cowered at the dark clouds looming overhead. The moment the British actor, William Charles Macready, appeared on stage, the opera house resounded with the spectators' jeers and hisses. Macready attempted to maintain his composure, until the audience began to pelt him with rotten eggs, the bombardment eventually driving him off the stage.

Following the commotion, Astor Place shut its doors temporarily until the scandal subsided. None in the opera house could foresee the cataclysm that would ensue when Astor decided to reopen its doors on the 10th of May. What started as a scuffle developed to a full-fledged riot involving up to 10,000 men, eventually claiming at least 25 lives and injuring another 120.

A depiction of the riot

By the end of what has since been memorialized as the "Astor Place Riot," a bold line divided the entertainment of New York according to class. To prevent history from repeating itself, citizens were encouraged to stay in their own lanes. Opera remained reserved for the upper and upper middle classes, whereas the middle to lower middle classes became patrons of melodramas and minstrel shows. Last, but not least, the poor attended and organized their own amateur variety shows in alleys, taverns, and venues of the like.

The Broadway theatre scene continued to flourish in the years that followed. Even more new genres generated by ingenious minds were unleashed onto the Broadway stages. In 1868, Eliza Hodges Thompson, along with her troupe, the British Blondes, titillated American audiences with the art of Victorian burlesque.

Contrary to what one might imagine, the classily erotic stripteases most know and love today did not become commonplace in the genre until the 20th century. Rather, the first form of "burlesque," which meant "to parody," was a blend of satirical plays, musicals, and different dances. Thompson, a trained ballet dancer, was well-versed in a myriad of dance styles, which shaped her shows with an unparalleled edge. She challenged more norms by excelling in male drag and dressing her ladies in skimpy clothing, shocking audiences and spiking ticket sales simultaneously.

Then, there was Tony Pastor, advertised as "the greatest clown and comic singer of the age," and to others, the supposed "Father of Vaudeville." Entertainment was all Pastor had known, for he had been shoved into the industry since the age of 6, where he donned the hats of circus acts, minstrelsy, any many others, even once appearing as a child prodigy in P.T. Barnum's American Museum in New York. In 1865, 28-year-old Pastor tried his hand at management by launching his own theatre and minstrel troupe, which was to become the resident cast of the Tony Pastor's Variety Show. That same year, he acquired the Bowery Music Hall and turned it into to Tony Pastor's Opera House.

16 years later, Pastor added yet another base to his growing entertainment network – the 14th Street Theatre, "the first specialty and Vaudeville theatre of America...catering to polite tastes, aiming to amuse, and fully up to current times and topics." In a nutshell, Vaudeville was variety entertainment, composed of snappy, but diverse talents such as singers, dancers, magicians, comedians, acrobats, contortionists, and other electrifying acts that packed a punch. The classic vaudeville show comprised up to 13 acts a time, most of which referenced pop culture and poked fun at current events.

Normally, vaudeville acts were geared towards male audiences due to their vulgar nature, but Pastor made it a point to capture the untouched female market by filtering out the lewdness and "purifying" his acts. When Pastor's "wholesome" brand of Vaudeville proved to be a home-run with the masses, jostling theatre managers hustled to follow the tracks of Pastor's footsteps. In 1874, the 14th Street Theatre was transferred to 585 Broadway, but when the expanding theatre district shifted towards Union Square, Pastor wisely moved his operations uptown.

The knockout successes of the multiplying theatres only inspired more to explore and modernize new fields of the art, further prolonging the catalog of theatrical genres and sub-genres. One of the most fashionable sub-genres of comedy at the time was the farce, which usually involved exciting, "highly improbable" story lines enlivened by physical humor. Another that fell under the musical comedy category was the pantomime, which was similar to "story theatre." Pantomime performers incorporated slapstick routines, jokes, and audience interaction set to music, and were perfect for reenacting silly children's stories.

Then, there was the far darker, but nonetheless widely embraced style of variety entertainment – the infamous minstrel shows. Minstrel shows consisted of variety acts, comic skits, songs, and dances that aimed at ridiculing minorities with grotesque caricatures that relied on hackneyed stereotypes. Slaves were almost always the butt of the joke, but were ironically, banned from setting foot on the stage until much later. The 1850s saw a particular upsurge in the leasing of minstrel halls.

In 1891, Charles H. Hoyt's comedy, A Trip to Chinatown opened at Broadway's Madison Square Theatre and proceeded to run for 657 performances, dogearing another page in history as the longest-running Broadway musical at the time.

By the mid-19th century, the stigma against actors – a profession once regarded as immoral and a magnet for eccentrics– had more or less receded. In fact, more and more leaders, politicians, and other illustrious names were giving acting a try. Those that mastered a niche or made a name for themselves in the industry became esteemed as honorable members of society.

Though glitz and glamor became synonymous with the entertainment industry, life as an actor, actress, or theatrical performer in general, was anything but a breeze. Quite the opposite, it involved arduous hard work that tested the limits of one's physical stamina. On top of a taxing schedule, which often required at least 3 cycles of rehearsals daily, actors were constantly being shuffled around in random lodges, and lost several hours due to travel each day.

The workload only intensified before and after the Civil War, as demand for more plays continued to soar to new heights. The average utility actor, which ranked lowest in the theatrical hierarchy, knew at least 100 parts by heart, and were expected to consume and learn new scripts within 2 days. For their services, utility actors were paid anywhere between $7 to $15 a week, whereas resident stars and lead actors commanded between $35 to $100. Touring actors were rewarded with the fattest paychecks of them all, which ranged from anywhere between $150 to $500 for week-long contracts.

The 19th century saw the highest rate of child actors in the history of theatre, many of whom rose to fame for playing characters up to 3 times their age. In this "free-thinking" environment, actresses also possessed a certain status that was unprecedented given the time period. Be that as it may, women still received lower salaries than their male counterparts.

The Exchange Comes to Wall Street

"The terrible, cold, cruel part is Wall Street. Rivers of gold flow there from all over the earth, and death comes with it. There, as nowhere else, you feel a total absence of the spirit: herds of men who cannot count past 3..." – Federico Garcia Lorca, Spanish poet

Wall Street in the 1780s

In 1790, Philadelphia founded the country's first ever stock exchange. The Board of Brokers from the Philadelphia Merchant's Exchange initially held their meetings in the City Tavern. With the blossoming populace of the city, the brokers knew they would soon outgrow the London Coffee House quarters. So, they set out to build their own headquarters from scratch. On the corner joining Second and Walnut Street, wealthy merchants, vessel captains, and other wealthy individuals teamed up to build an opulent 4-story building capped with handsome multiple gable roofs and dozens of rooms.

Finally, the Philadelphia Merchant's Exchange was open for business. A business card from the innkeeper during its opening year described what was to be expected at the new tavern. The 2 large conference rooms in the front of the establishment were open to brokers for use from noon to 2PM, and 6 to 8 in the evening. In the tavern, one could enjoy the stable, newly furnished rooms, and have some grub and drink at the bar, all of which came at "reasonable rates." Later, in 1865, the Board of Brokers rebranded the merchant's exchange as the Philadelphia Stock Exchange.

Back in New York, early stock brokers claimed their territory on Wall Street. The meetings of early brokers transpired in the cool shade of a buttonwood tree. Here, merchants auctioned off stocks from banks and mines, and received commissions of 0.25% from every successful sale. The spirited chatter from hustling merchants in the open-air exchange could be heard throughout the block of 68 Wall Street. Shortly after, they began to conduct their daily meetings at the Tontine Coffee House, which were held twice a day.

A depiction of the buttonwood tree

1797 oil on linen of the Tontine Coffee House, Merchant's Coffee House, and Wall Street, leading down to the East River, by Francis Guy (1760–1820)

In 1789, George Washington was sworn in as the first president at Federal Hall, located along Wall Street, and 3 years later, 24 influential merchants crafted The Buttonwood Agreement. It was a pact promising to bar government intervention from their open-air market, and to shun away all newcomers. The only way outsiders could purchase stock was to go through an approved broker. Following the agreement, the merchants moved to a rented room on 40 Wall Street, effectively excluding themselves from the public eye.

Hearing of the thriving Philadelphia Merchant's Exchange, Wall Street authorities dispatched observers to the state. When the observers returned and relayed the information they learned to their superiors, the New York Stock and Exchange Board came to fruition on March 8, 1817. They later shortened the name to the New York Stock Exchange in 1863. Word traveled through the grapevine, and Wall Street became known as the auction block for slaves.

Along with slave auctions, Wall Street became notorious for enforcing public humiliation. Prisoners, many of which had committed the crime of perjury, had their necks and wrists cuffed by wooden pillories. Mobs of people attended the public humiliations to jeer and hurl rotten vegetables at the shackled prisoners.

In 1817, the NYSE formed their own constitution protecting their exclusivity, and laid a fixed schedule in place. Each morning started off with Anthony Stockholm, president of the board, reciting the stocks available for trade. To obtain a seat in the hush-hush club, one had to be voted in. The potential candidate can also be refused by 3 non-consenting votes. A seat on the exchange cost $25 (approximately $441 USD buying power today). Just a decade later, the price ballooned to $100 ($1,763 USD). By 1848, it was at $400 a pop. The private club even had their own uniforms – a wardrobe of top hats and dark swallowtail coats.

As years passed, the New York Merchant Group realized their stock exchange was failing. This came as a consequence of plunging war bonds and stocks in the Bank of the United States. At this time, only 30 companies held a place in the exchange. These included reputable banks, construction firms, and cargo companies.   Buyers were limited to what historians described as "fearless investors." They were thought of as gamblers, filthy rich, or had intentions of taking over a company. The average individual was terrified of stocks, as the bankruptcy of a company meant stock owners could blow their life savings completely. Uninvited brokers, otherwise known as "curbstone brokers," were left to trade less reputable stocks on the streets, where disagreements often led to a couple of punches or full-out brawls. They later formed their own exchange, dubbing it the American Stock Exchange.

Most importantly, the club's exclusivity was only throttling business. They needed to keep up with the times, as the rest of the world was allowing anyone to join the market. The only advantage from keeping it a private club was that the fixed number of brokers could regulate themselves, thereby avoiding fraud. Begrudgingly, the NYSE opened its doors to the public once more.

Wall Street in 1829

Depiction of Wall Street in 1825 and 1829

When the exchange's rented office at 40 Wall Street was destroyed by a fire that engulfed the entire building in 1835, the board relocated to an office on 10-12 Street. There they stayed until the end of the 19th century, moving when the members outgrew that office, too. By then, with the help of the westward expansion, business at the stock exchange had flourished.

The New York Stock Exchange in the 1880s

Architect George B. Post was assigned to design the new building, the very same that stands today. Construction began in May of 1901. The old buildings from 10-12 Street were scrapped to make way for the new building. During construction, passersby marveled at the looming Corinthian pillars and the brilliant neoclassical facade. The Piccirilli Brothers were in charge of crafting the pediment, with the sculptures featured molded by John Quincy Adams Ward. When it was finished, they christened the pediment "Integrity Protecting the Works of Man." $4 million and 2 years later, construction concluded. On April 22, 1903, the office was officially open.

At 109 x 140 feet, coupled with a ceiling that hovered 72 feet off the ground, the trading floor was one of the largest spaces the 20th century had ever seen. The interior was equally majestic, with the walls and floors covered with sleek marble. The rooms were cooled with the first ever air-conditioning system, an invention that had been introduced to the world just a year before. In the hopes of creating a pleasant atmosphere, brokers were greeted with perfumed air pumped out of the ventilation system. Stock certificates were safely kept in the hundreds of secure vaults underground. The stocks were treated like inventories and sold like every other over-the-counter product.

20ᵗʰ century pictures of the interior

Technology played a critical role in the steady expansion of Wall Street. When Baron Pavel Schilling invented the telegraph in 1832, the world of finance was never the same. Information could now be spread across the country faster than ever before. Samuel Morse brought the invention to the United States, and in 1837, he launched a demonstration office for the telegraph on Wall Street, just a few doors down from the stock exchange. He charged brokers 25 cents apiece for a peek at the new invention. Brokers were giddy with excitement, passing on the word to everyone they knew. Gone were those days when brokers had to physically walk across the trading floor to search for a single deal.

Before long, Wall Street was festooned with telegraph wires weaving down the blocks. The stock exchange welcomed the telegraph with open arms, a fitting new tool for their free-for-all system. By extinguishing the need for other regional markets around the country, New York became the financial capital of the United States.

In 1867, brokers readily embraced the next technological innovation by Edward A. Calahan from The American Telegraph Company – the stock ticker. Stock tickers were bulky machines with a wheel of ticker tape attached to the top. Ticker tapes were narrow paper strips that were threaded through the machine. The ticker printed abbreviated names of companies, along with volume information and stock transaction prices. As the machine printed, it made a rhythmic ticking sound, which was how the machine earned its name.

With every sale, a clerk would roll up a sheet with the details of the transaction and insert it into a pneumatic tube. These tubes sucked up the paper rolls, zipping through the pipe-like system before reaching its destination at the ticker tape room. Typists were then tasked with releasing the information to the rest of the world. With the aid of the stock ticker and telegraph lines, brokers across the country could be updated with up-to-the-minute prices. Best of all, those beyond the doors of the once clandestine exchange could fully understand what was going on.

On July 8, 1889, *The Wall Street Journal* sold its very first issue at a price of 2 cents per paper. Thanks to Charles Dow, Charles Bergstresser, and Edward Jones of Dow Jones & Company, the famed newspaper altered the face of journalism. Many sprung out of their beds to get their hands on the paper, flipping the page to its most important feature. Known as the "Dow-Jones Industrial Average," it was an index of 12 stocks, their performance graphed by the month. The 12 stocks included some of the country's largest corporations including US Rubber, American Sugar, and General Electric.

Dow

As Wall Street slowly took over the world of finance over the years, they soon developed their own slang. The most frequently heard of the lingo are the "Bulls" and the "Bears." Once used as nicknames for speculators, they are now terms for different stock markets. Bear markets are tainted and often associated with negativity, leading to bubbles and other economic declines. They were given the nickname for its historical significance. Ancient bearskin traders were known for selling their products before actually receiving the supply. They crossed their fingers, hoping for a downturn in the market so they could walk away with larger profits. On the contrary, "Bulls" refer to a positive, upward-trending market, where investor confidence is at its highest. Furthermore, stocks with under-performing stocks or assets are referred to as "Dogs."

"Wolves" are ranked on the top of the pyramid. These powerful investors are considered the hotshots of Wall Street. Ferocious wolves are bloodthirsty investors who would stop at nothing to get to the top, sometimes succumbing to criminal means to get their way. In other countries, these investors are known as "Sharks" or "Tigers."

Next, came the "Ostriches." These are wishful thinkers who fail to act during critical changes in the market. Like the animal, Ostriches dig their heads under the sand, ignoring the news as they pray for better days ahead. Ostriches are also known to go MIA when the market gets tough.

Then, there are the "Pigs." Pigs are investors blinded by greed, resorting to unethical strategies for their deals. These investors are not satisfied with 100% returns, and would borrow money for margins to buy more stocks at higher prices for an even larger profit.

Animal terms are also used for choices investors make on the market. "Sheep" are investors with no strategies or clear paths ahead. They rely on financial advice from others like sheep to a shepherd. Because of their inability to think for themselves, they miss out on opportunities other shrewd investors pounce on. Sheep investors are often mauled by the Bulls and Bears of Wall Street. On that note, ineffective investors are also called "Lame Ducks," characterized by their tendency to "waddle" out of the market. Lame Duck businesses are those that go bankrupt or default on their debts.

In later years, more terms were added to the list of Wall Street lingo. Start-up businesses less than 5 years old valued at over a billion dollars with no stock market history are deemed "Unicorns." "Dragons" are similar to "Unicorns," as these businesses generated more than 100% of investments. "Black Swans" are unpredictable events, even with the help of some of the most elaborate investment models. "Stags," or "Flipping," are traders that buy into a company's IPO (initial public offering). Taking advantage of the rising prices on the market, they sell these shares straight away.

Last, but not least, there is the morbidly termed "Dead Cat Bounce." The almost literal term describes the specific market trend exactly, in which there is a temporary spike in stock prices after a devastating fall. As the Oxford English Dictionary puts it, "If you throw a dead cat against a wall at a high rate of speed, it will bounce, but it is still dead."

With all these terms in mind, there is no wonder why so many call Wall Street "The Jungle."

Black Broadway

"I have never been able to discover that there was anything disgraceful in being a colored man, but I have often found it inconvenient." – Bert Williams

Black-face minstrelsy remains one of the most atrocious segments of American history, and rightfully so. It was Thomas Dartmouth Rice, better known as his stage name, "Daddy," who was said to have played the first character in black-face on a Broadway stage. Rice, who had dressed himself down with tattered rags and smeared his face, neck, and hands with burnt cork, made his first appearance as "Jim Crow," a friendly, but dumbed down slave cursed with 2 left feet. Jim Crow became such a sensation that the "separate but equal" laws that were later used to segregate the blacks and whites, was named after the character.

A depiction of Rice as Jim Crow

Before the Civil War, whites, mainly in the South, circulated racist disinformation in the hopes of squashing the abolitionist message. The slaves in their plays were depicted as lost, substandard souls that needed slavery to keep them civilized. Additionally, the characters were often terrified of what lay beyond the plantation, and shunned their freedoms for a life of labor and servitude, for it was all they knew. During this time, African Americans were barred from the stage by law, but managers that sympathized with the abolitionist cause often hired black actors behind closed doors, some of whom were slipped paychecks under the table.

The end of the war saw the emergence of exclusively black minstrel companies, but even so, African Americans were still made to "blackify" themselves so they could be "dark enough" for the audience. African American actors grudgingly slathered thick coats of greasepaint and shoe polish onto their skins. Some painted their mouths and the area around it to exaggerate the size of their lips. All were made to slur their speech with "plantation accents" and play up various and untruthful clichés about their own race. Still, many, such as William Henry Lane, the inventor tap dancing, sucked it up, as for most African Americans, it was their only shot at performing on a professional stage.

In spite of the backlash received by the black community and some of their educated white brethren, the black-face tradition was one that continued well into the 1900s, and is still occasionally used in poorly thought out costumes for 21st century parties today. One of the most vehement and vocal critics of black-face was Frederick Douglass, a former slave, gifted orator, and abolitionist leader in the states of New York and Massachusetts. Douglass harangued its propagators in an aggressive, but eloquent speech, describing them as the "filthy scum of white society, who have stolen from us a complexion denied to them by nature, in which to make money, and pander to the corrupt taste of their fellow white citizens."

Of course, it comes as no shocker that the only road made accessible to the African Americans in theatre was one filled with double the abrupt turns and obstacles, and finished off by a staircase with steps spaced so far apart, clambering onto the next level was next to impossible.

In response to the exclusion, William Henry Brown, a former ship steward of black and West Indian descent, pieced together his own "pleasure garden" back in 1821. This gathering place, which was situated at his backyard in Thomas Street, became the first African American-owned venue that allowed entry to and granted stage time to those rich in melanin. The animated music and soulful vocals that poured out into the streets pricked the ears of the curious.

That same year, Brown mustered together the first African American theatre troupe – the African Company – and established the African Grove Theatre on Broadway's Mercer Street. Brown had purchased a modest but charming building attached to a tea garden. The top floor of the 2-story structure was then converted to a playhouse that held up to 300 seats. On the 21st of September, the African Company inaugurated its new season with a polished performance of Richard III, and unlike the white-only playhouses, welcomed white attendees. Other plays included in their program were other Shakespearean works such as Othello, as well as William Moncrieff's Life in London, and the French comedy, Dom Juan, as adapted by Molière.

2 years later, The Drama of King Shotaway, the first African American play, written and arranged by Brown, premiered on the African Grove stage. The story, which was centered on the 1796 Black Carib War in St. Vincent, was poignantly told by 45-year-old James Hewlett, who is often credited with being the first black Shakespearean Thespian. Another shining member of the cast was 16-year-old Ira Aldridge, who, along with Hewlett and many other actors in the African

Company, experienced their first brush with the craft by sneaking into the Park Theatre and other playhouses in the city.

At the outset, amused authorities and media humored Brown when they learned that he, together with his all-black entourage, were taking on Shakespeare. That was, until Brown's performers began to truly conquer that field, promptly wiping the smirks off their faces. Thugs employed by rival theatre owners attempted to storm into the African Grove Theatre to interrupt its programs. In the end, a white judge decreed that Brown's Company put a stop to Shakespearean performances altogether. Though the African Company abided by the decree, they had evidently ruffled some feathers, and as a result, suffered harassment until they were forced to disband in late 1823.

Activity in Black Broadway might have been stalled until after the Civil War, but Brown's victories, which motivated many of his brothers and sisters across the color spectrum, had helped to foster its progress. Towards the late 19th and early 20th centuries, Black Broadway experienced something of a golden era. African American artists invented new genres of music and nurtured the development of their own culture, and many began to make strides in the industry.

The African American communities along the Midwest, chiefly in Missouri, created ragtime, a brand of jaunty and "springy" music typically played on the piano. Ragtime, derived from the term "ragged time," was a predecessor to jazz music, distinguishable by its broken and "ragged," yet bouncy melodies. It has been described as a relative of the "cakewalk," a complex, but graceful style of dance performed by slaves to please their masters in the plantations; they then received a wedge of cake as a "treat." The music of the slaves was later borrowed – or stolen, depending on how one looks at it – post-slavery by white musicians such as John Philip Sousa and Russell Bennett.

In 1893, the American public at the Chicago World's Fair was blessed with these cheerful tunes – which they referred to as "coon music" – for the first time. Ragtime slipped into the Black Broadway scene in no time, accompanied by satirical plays and parodies of black speech and thought. Among these "coon song" parodies was one entitled "All Coons Look Alike to Me," written by one of the earliest African American Broadway producers and performers, Ernest Hogan. It was also the first appearance of the "rag" style on sheet music.

Hogan went on to amass over $26,000, for the song was the equivalent of a Billboard 100 topper of its time, but it would not take long before remorse began to set in. "All Coons Look Alike," "Coon Song," and the satirical messages behind other lampoons were lost with white audiences. The public took this as a green light to heighten the white people's derision of blacks. They created and prolonged damaging stereotypes, including the African American community's fondness for chicken and watermelon, and portrayed their men as volatile, alcoholic, sex addicts. In an interview, Hogan claimed that a woman had quoted his own song to him when rejecting his advances.

Nevertheless, African Americans continued to strive for recognition in the scene under a system built against them. Scott Joplin, often praised as the "King of Ragtime," was another character to do just that. Joplin, who composed "The Entertainer," one of the most recognizable tunes of the 20th century, often used in comedic bar fights (as well as the theme song to the '70s flick, The Sting) was particularly paranoid about how his white critics would view his ragtime music, as it had come from a black man. Determined for ragtime to be taken seriously, he published a comprehensive book that took apart and examined the genre for first-time learners, entitled The School of Ragtime: Six Exercises for Piano.

Joplin had firsthand experience when it came to being stiffed on deal, not due to his lack of talent, but the shade of his skin. When he released "Original Rags," his first "piano rag" in print, it was said that he had reluctantly been made to share the glory with a white arranger, Charles N. Daniels. Whether or not Daniels had actually played a part in the process remains in dispute. Disgruntled but undeterred, Joplin hired a lawyer and drew up a contract that guaranteed him a cent for every print sold of his next work, "The Maple Leaf Rag." The single eventually drummed up so much interest, over a million copies were sold.

Meanwhile, more black thespians and musicians were breaking free from their molds. In 1897, Bob Cole, a composer, director, producer, performer, and overall jack-of-all-trades in the theatre business, became the first black man to write a musical farce – A Trip to Coontown. It was also the first musical almost entirely created, managed, cast, and performed by African Americans. The dark plot, which followed a street swindler as he attempts to con an elderly man into handing over everything he owned, was lightened by a "carnivalesque atmosphere," and featured yet another first. Fans of black-face were given a taste of their own medicine when Cole, as the tramp, "Willy Wayside," strutted onto the stage, his face painted pasty-white and his beard dyed red.

Then, there was Bert Williams, one of the biggest and most respected names to ever come out of Vaudeville. His name made its first splash in 1895 as the other half of a comic duo, his partner another African-American actor by the name of George Walker. Walker's character was the ying to Bert's yang, a quick-witted, mouthy fellow from the city versus a dim, but well-meaning "country bumpkin."

In 1903, the pair starred in In Dahomey, the first all-black musical to make it to the Broadway stage. Williams later went on to become not just a permanent cast member, but the main feature of Florenz Ziegfeld's Follies, shattering another ceiling by becoming the first black Broadway star to perform as an "equal alongside whites." Though the Bahamian-American was a natural under the spotlight, the pressure of constantly being the odd one out took its toll on him. Comedian W.C. Fields of the silent film era once made the rueful remark that Williams was "the funniest man [he] ever saw, and the saddest."

Williams caked on black makeup as he was expected to before stepping onto the stage, but he made it a point to never sell himself out for the amusement of the whites. He chose roles relatable to audiences of any color, and took parts that depicted black characters in everyday situations. Even so, not everyone was as eager to share the stage with Williams.

White actors at the time were not shy to voice their discontent with Williams' name on the playbill, and at times, threatened to walk out if Williams was not recast. His celebrity meant nothing to many hotels and restaurants he was a patron of, and was still often made to dine alone, ride on separate elevators, among other trivial yet meaningful inconveniences. Williams once lamented, "It wouldn't be so bad...if I didn't hear the applause still ringing in my ears."

About 2 years after Williams' death, Paul Robeson, a former football player and law graduate of Columbia University, took to the Broadway stage in the 1924 play All God's Chillun Got Wings. Robeson's deep, silvery voice made him an immediate favorite of the critics, but his character, who was wedded to a white woman, stirred up a storm of letters from the protesting public. Robeson refused to be defeated by his naysayers, and instead, used their vilification of him as fuel to scurry up the rings on the ladder of success. In 1943, Robeson was awarded the lead role in Othello, effectively shutting up his critics when the play went on to run for another 295 shows. It was at that point, the longest-running Shakespearean Broadway production of all time.

Ups, Downs, and the Great White Way

"Give my regards to Broadway, remember me to Herald Square. Tell all the gang at 42nd Street, that I will soon be there..." – "Give My Regards to Broadway," lyrics by George M. Cohan

Broadway north from 38ᵗʰ St. in the early 20ᵗʰ century

In the early 20ᵗʰ century, A. L. Erlanger and Marcus Klaw were commissioned to construct what would become known as the New Amsterdam Theatre on 42ⁿᵈ Street. The building was built with a blend of Beaux-Arts and Art Nouveau, a style of architecture popularized in France, distinctive for its use of elegant swirls, curvature, rounded, curled lettering, and "plant-like gates." The slender, but ornate facade gave visitors only a taste of the grandeur that lay inside. A majestic arch garlanded with flowers and scrolls, and headlined by the statues of Cupid; Drama; a Knight; a Lady, and Pierrot, the sad clown, was sculpted over the entrance. Striking yellow columns with bronze embellishments stood guard on either side of the doors.

As stunning as its facade was, what was inside was what took the visitors' breaths away. First and foremost, the narrowness of the theatre's entrance was misleading. The auditorium inside, decked out with 1,702 seats, stretched out to 41st Street, making it the largest in all of New York in its day. The lobby featured a floor tiled with clay, a crackling fireplace, marble wall fountains decorated with technicolor mosaics, and bronze statues of the most eminent figures in theatre. On the roof was another theatre that would be open to the public in the summertime.

Upon entering the auditorium, guests were greeted by a clear, yet delicately subtle floral theme that pervaded the interior in harmonious shades of teal, lilac, pink, red, and gold. "Pod-like boxes" projected from the walls with a nearly-panoramic view of the main floor. These balconies, occupied by the deluxe clientele, were garnished with its own set of flowers and vines in peach, purple, honey-gold, and butterscotch.

Once the finishing touches were applied, the opening date was set for October 25, 1902. That evening, the New Amsterdam Theatre presented A Midsummer Night's Dream to a packed house. An infatuated critic of architecture called the theatre upon his departure "the most airy, fairy beautiful thing in the way of a playhouse that the New York public has ever seen." It appeared as if the New Amsterdam Theatre had arrived just in time, for the New York theatre scene was on the cusp of a monumental transformation.

The New Amsterdam Theatre in the early 20th century

In the last years of the 19th century, a new headquarters for the New York Times, then headed by Adolph S. Ochs, was ordered, which was to be erected on Longacre Square's 42nd Street. As construction of the skyscraper transpired, Ochs talked the city's mayor into building a subway station there. On April 8, 1904, just a few months away from the headquarters' completion, Longacre Square was rebranded "Times Square."

The 25-story "wedge-shaped" skyscraper towered over the city, complete with state-of-the-art printing press facilities in its basement, and a private observatory on the rooftop reserved for the Ochs family. The publishing company commemorated its opening day on New Year's Eve that year with an astounding fireworks display, illuminating a massive sign that read "1905" perched upon the top of the tower. An excerpt from the paper published the following day reminisced, "No more beautiful picture was ever limned in fire on the curtain of midnight." Ochs was even more chuffed to hear of the success of the newly installed New York subway line, which was receiving rave reviews. At 7 in the evening of its opening day, over 100,000 New Yorkers teemed into the Manhattan subway station to test out the mass transit system at a nickel a head.

With Times Square now more accessible than ever, it became the beating heart of American arts and culture, home to Broadway's theatres, music halls, swanky restaurants, upscale hotels, and other establishments of the elite. It was here that in 1917, O.J. Gude, a dynamite in publicity and the "Sign King of Times Square," set up a block-long billboard for Wrigley's between Broadway's 43rd and 44th Streets. The gigantic billboard, or a "spectacular," as it was called, was one of over 10,000 Gude originals. It stood 8 stories tall and 200-ft in length, spangled with 17,500 lights that bathed the once inky-black streets with an enchanting white glow.

When just about every storefront on Times Square adopted the brilliant advertising tactic, the distinguished neighborhood landed itself a new nickname – the Great White Way. At this point, white bulbs were exclusively used, as colored bulbs fizzled out at twice the speed. The Red Mill, a musical set in modern times, which was among the most popular genres of the era, was the first Broadway show to entice potential audiences with a spectacular.

In 1927, the journalist Will Irwin painted a picture of the incredible scene: "Mildly insane by day, the square goes divinely mad by night. For then on every wall, above every cornice, in every nook and cranny, blossom and dance the electric advertising signs...All other American cities imitate them, but none gets this massed effect of tremendous jazz interpreted in light." Even better, it was around this time that the Actors Equity Association decreed that it be absolutely necessary for all actors to sign standard contracts safeguarding their rights in the workplace prior to every season of a professional production. To thespian hopefuls everywhere, Broadway had never looked so appetizing.

Just as it seemed as if the theatre industry was set for another explosion, Broadway stumbled into a slump. It was none other than the introduction of sound in motion pictures around the end of the 1920s that sounded the alarm bells at Broadway. Live Vaudeville could not ignore the loud and seemingly permanent arrival of cinema, and found many of its biggest stars seduced to the other side. This had critics and pessimists stroking their chins as they wondered if they were in fact, witnessing the murder of live theatre.

But Broadway was not going to kowtow so easily. Among the most notable names to spearhead the fight for the theatre scene's survival was Florenz Ziegfeld. The Follies, the hallmark of Ziegfeld's career, was one of the most successful theatrical revues – a type of multi-act entertainment filled with musical numbers and sketches – in Broadway history. The Ziegfeld girls were enough to lure the audience into the New Amsterdam Theatre, which came to be their regular venue, on a regular basis.

Ziegfeld's chorus girls were composed of the most exquisite (albeit predominantly white) and talented ladies in the United States, dolled up in twinkling costumes and jewelry. These women were required to complete a grueling training process, for they were often made to balance extravagant and extremely heavy headdresses as they glided down the steps and sashayed from one end of the stage to the other. The enormity of the venue also allowed for Ziegfeld's sumptuous sets, which came with resplendent and outstandingly detailed backdrops, made even more imposing by the finest stage equipment and sound system in the business.

Olive Thomas was one of Ziegfeld's most adored chorus girls. The fair-complexioned, raven-haired stunner was treasured for her arresting eyes and perfect pout, and lauded for her natural talent on stage and behind the camera lens. Following her untimely death in 1920, staff at the New Amsterdam Theatre reported multiple sightings of the troubled beauty, her spectral figure still clad in her favorite Follies costume – a bottle-green, beaded number – with a blue flask clutched in hand.

Thomas

Another influential thespian to rise to prominence during this time was Eugene O'Neill. He became the first American playwright to be awarded the Nobel prize for literature, as well as another 4 Pulitzer wins for drama under his belt, for he steered the ship of Broadway towards the unfamiliar, but promising waters of drama. Deciding that farces and melodramas were inundating an industry in danger of going stale, O'Neill introduced "psychological and social realism" to the Broadway stage, often pinning the focus of his stories on minorities and other groups slighted by society. His love for drama was documented in his body of work – of over 50 plays written by O'Neill, only one, Ah, Wilderness!, was a comedy, and even then, it was abundantly peppered with elements of prostitution, alcoholism, revenge, and stifled desires. O'Neill's stamp in Broadway history is well-defined, for he is said to have served as the muse for Tennesse Williams, Sam Shepard, and other stage pioneers.

Between 1933 and 1942, Broadway slid deeper into its rut, its culprit the withering strike of the Great Depression. Broadway was not immune to the stock market crash, which saw even Ziegfeld and other stars of the like descending into a bout of panic. Business was so abysmal that even the New Amsterdam Theatre was forced to shut its doors in 1936.

It became even more difficult to keep up with Hollywood, which was quickly snatching up Broadway's hallowed stars, with one source placing the number of Broadway-to-Hollywood converts at 75%. Throughout the extent of this Broadway black age, theatres were either eerily empty, or partially filled on a good day. As a comparison, the Broadway seasons between 1929 to 1930 produced 233 shows. Between 1930 to 1931, that number dropped to 187.

Thankfully, this dry spell was short-lived. Towards the end of the 1940s, Broadway had won back its prestige, and then some. Prior to the comeback, not a single Broadway show had broken the record of 500. The country folk drama, Oklahoma!, arranged by Oscar Hammerstein II and composer Richard Rodgers, had garnered a total of 2,212 shows by the end of its run. The talented twosome has since been credited with resurrecting Broadway from the dead.

Many had cheered for Broadway's revival, for it had earned many fans at an unlikely time – the Second World War. Broadway had never made their liberal views a secret, but it strove far and beyond to display their patriotism. Many in Broadway pitched in to help wherever they could, some departing to enlist in the war, while others stayed behind to improve public morale with comedy sketches. In 1942, the Shubert Brothers, remembered as the sovereigns to the "largest theatre empire in the 20th century," converted the 44th Street Theatre to the "Stage Door Canteen." This was a much-needed place of solace for the soldiers on break from their tours, where they were entertained with music and shows, and snacked on pies, sandwiches, roast meats, coffee, and cakes donated by the public.

In 1947, the American Theatre Wing developed an awards show as a salute to the most paramount names in theatre, which they called the "Tony Awards." The program was named as such as an homage to Antoinette Perry, a director, actress, and as Time put it, "the wartime guiding spirit" of the Wing, who had died the year before. The first awards ceremony was set for April 6, 1947 in the Grand Ballroom of the Waldorf Astoria Hotel.

Though the dress code was black tie optional, every celebrity in attendance was dressed to impress. Vera Allen, the newly appointed chairwoman of the Wing, played host for the evening. Ethel Waters, Mickey Rooney, and David Wayne were among the names in the roster for the night, and 11 actors and actresses went home with Tonys presented in 7 categories.

An Act of Terror

"I saw the explosion, a column of smoke shoot up into the air and then saw people dropping all around me, some of them with their clothing afire." – Charles P. Dougherty, stock exchange messenger

With the brand new facilities and all the technological advances on Wall Street, business was running smoothly. Following World War I, J.P. Morgan and Company made its name on the legendary street as well. This Goliath of a bank became the most influential institution of its kind in the world. A stroll across the street and one would find the US Sub-Treasury and the Assay Office. And just a few buildings down the road, the hectic commotion from the always-full stock exchange spilled out into the streets. All seemed well.

But just 17 years later after the New York Stock Exchange opened its doors, tragedy struck. It was September 16, 1920. Light showers were expected for the day, but the sidewalks were teeming with brokers, clerks, and other members of the lunchtime crowd hurrying for a quick bite to eat. The streets were jammed with automobiles caught in traffic. Alongside them were a chain of messenger boys on bicycles, blowing raspberries as they waited for the snail-paced traffic to move along.

With an air of impatience gripping the annoyed lunchtime crowd, no one bothered to take a second glance at the mysterious vehicle parked out front of the Assay Office. A shabby horse-drawn wagon sat next to the curb. Taking advantage of the oblivious crowd, the driver of the wagon quietly released the horse reins. Then, the faceless driver hopped off the wagon and slithered into the crowd, making a clean escape down the street before vanishing around the corner.

When the hands of the clock touched noon, the bells from Trinity Church rang across Wall Street. But before the final chime sounded at 12:01, the wagon exploded. In one split second, a thunderous roar blasted through the streets. The sudden blast shook the earth, so powerful it derailed a car a full block down. It propelled the doomed car to the 34th floor of the Equitable Building before it came crashing back to the ground.

The wind quickly carried the roaring billows of flame and dense, pitch-black smoke down the streets. Shrapnel, glass, metal, debris, and bloody chunks of human and horse parts rained from the skies. Andrew Dunn, an employee of J.P. Morgan and Co, was a witness who was lucky enough to escape the blast. He recalled, "That was the loudest noise I ever heard in my life. It was enough to knock you out by itself." Even Joseph P. Kennedy, father of President John F. Kennedy, who was present at the bombing, remembered being flung off his feet by the mere force of the blast.

The wreckage and aftermath of the wagon dynamite can only be described as utter pandemonium. Buildings were wholly destroyed, with one of the casualties being the J.P. Morgan building. Those who were close to the detonation were burnt to crisps, adding the nauseating stench of burning flesh and hair to the screaming frenzy. Some lost their lives or were severely injured, crushed by the debris of crumbling buildings.

A picture after the bombing

In order to achieve maximum damage, the perpetrators piled dozens of iron sash weights on top of the bomb. These weights were narrow, flute-like objects that were used to weigh down the sashes on sash windows. One could be as heavy as 30 lbs. When the weights exploded along with the bomb, a great many were sliced up from the jagged pieces of the lethal shrapnel.

All trading at Wall Street immediately screeched to a halt. Over 2,000 New York City policemen and Red Cross nurses flooded the scene to contain the chaos. Hundreds were burned and maimed, some beyond recognition. 30 civilians were killed on the spot, and another 8 would later succumb to their injuries. Until the Oklahoma City bombing that would take place 75 years later, the Wall Street explosion was the deadliest to date.

When the streets were cleared, investigators began the hunt for the bombers. Though they had no leads on who exactly had orchestrated the bombing, they were certain the target was the J.P. Morgan bank. Some believed those responsible were resentful of the alleged profits the bank made off the devastation of the First World War, but the majority of the victims were made up of low-level clerks and stenographers. J.P. Morgan Jr., the believed target, was off vacationing in Europe at the time of the blast.

J.P. Morgan, Jr.

The *St. Louis Post-Dispatch*, however, claimed it was terrorism. They stated, "The bomb was not directed at any particular person or property. It was directed against a public, anyone who happened to be near or any property in the neighborhood."

A solid clue came a day later. Postal workers discovered flyers stuffed in the Financial District mailboxes. All bore the same message: "Remember, we will not tolerate any longer. Free the political prisoners, or it will be sure death for all of you." It was signed by the "American Anarchist Fighters." Investigators noticed the flyers' uncanny resemblance to those previously circulated on June of 1919. That terrifying year, the group set off a string of bombs in multiple American cities.

The police pinned the crime on the Galleanists. Led by Luigi Galleani, an authoritative speaker and explosives expert, the Galleanists were a dangerous gang of Italian anarchists with a deep-seated hatred for government. Even more incriminating, the Galleanists were infamous for using iron shaft weights for shrapnel in their explosives.

Since then, no other group has come forward to claim responsibility for the Wall Street attack. That said, an interesting facet of the case came with a mentally unsound tennis champion named Edward Fischer. Fischer was heard warning strangers to stay off Wall Street a few days before the attack. Authorities probed further, but were unable to connect him to the case. The Bureau of Investigation (known as the FBI today) proceeded to spend more than 3 years tracking down the assailants, but ultimately came up short.

To this day, the case remains ice-cold.

The Catastrophic Crash of 1929

Pictures of crowds gathering on Wall Street during the stock market crash

"The wires to other cities were jammed with frantic orders to sell... Buyers were few, sometimes wholly absent... This was real panic... When the closing bell rang, the great bull market was dead and buried." – Johnathan Norton Leonard, author of *Three Years Down*

After the Allied Powers victory in World War I, the mood shifted across the nation. The economy picked up, with more families willing to splurge on non-necessities. As factories around the country worked double-time to fill the new orders, it was a seemingly win-win situation for everyone who hitched a ride on the bandwagon. More and more households, particularly in the middle and lower class, indulged themselves with goods and services typically reserved for the upper class. When weekends came along, every seat in the new picture theaters was filled. Phonographs, record collections, and cars adorned the living rooms and garages of these households.

By the 1920s, business at the stock exchange was flowing peachily, and it continued to be the talk of the town. The brokers and clerks were among those in peppier spirits. They were not only grateful for the new facilities, they were pleased with the new, more organized system that came with it.

Each stock was now traded at assigned spots known as posts. Every post served stocks of a different nature, with railroad stocks found in one post and steel stocks in another. This made it easier for brokers to navigate the trading floor. Specialists, sometimes known as Auctioneers, were in charge of the bidding.

The soaring economy lifted the hopes of both Wall Street and the general public alike, continuing to do so over the 1920s. Harold Geneen, who was 16 when he started as a page on the trading floor back in 1926, spoke of his first impression on the stock exchange. He reminisced, "It was a very exuberant period. I thought it was kinda lively and a lot of fun."

The 1920s also opened Wall Street's doors to women. This was revolutionary, unheard of in the once all-boys club. Prior to this, gender prejudice was the only barrier that kept the women outside the Wall Street buildings. Women were thought to be incapable of rational decision-making on the scorching hot trading floor, and lacked the astute foresight men possessed for speculating in the market. But around the country, women were slowly making a stand for themselves. They began cropping up at colleges and unorthodox workplaces, and were now allowed to handle their own finances. Understandably, independent women began setting their eyes on Wall Street, looking to make riches of their own. With every passing year, the number of female Wall Street clerks swelled.

Along with the millions of household goods and the influx of cars sold across the country, the public themselves began to dip their toes in the murky pool of stock and investment. More curious Average Joes turned to the Wall Street Journal to analyze the stocks. They, too, started to purchase shares of their favorite companies, mostly those that made the goodies and cars they owned.

Even celebrities of the era were dabbling in stock investments. The public scoped out the investment activities of actors like celebrated silent-film star, Charlie Chaplin, and famous eyebrow-and-mustache combo, Julius "Groucho" Marx. Many began modeling their own investments after what Chaplin and Marx happened to be speculating on.

Marx was known for dumping all his savings into stock investments. After filming each scene, he would make a beeline for the phone, calling up his broker for updates. He was so delighted with the results, he convinced his brothers to do the same. Later, he shared his triumphs with the public, announcing on the papers, "What an easy racket. [Stock] went up 7 points since this morning. I just made myself $7,000!"

Sentiments like these encouraged the directionless public, but this was not Wall Street's first attempt to hone in on the untapped market. To spice up sales of war bonds during World War I, awareness events were hosted outside Wall Street buildings. Like charity concerts today, they featured a wide range of celebrities, predominantly stars from motion picture films. Alongside Chaplin, America's sweetheart, Martha Mansfield, and lovable tough guy, Douglas Fairbanks, addressed the crowd with conical megaphones. They riled up the public with patriotic speeches which were met with approving hoots and hollers. A gripping headline splashed across the 1918 issue of the New York Tribune read, "20,000 Throng Wall Street to Hear Movie Stars Tell How to Win War." Before these events, the public had no experience on purchasing stocks or bonds. They had no idea what they were getting themselves into.

With the rampant demand for stocks, prices skyrocketed. Between the years of 1924 and 1929, the Dow-Jones Industrial Average rose a whopping 300%. Unbeknownst to the vast majority of the public, a lava of turmoil was bubbling underneath them, and the ground was starting to crack. As Geneen said, "You had a lot of people in the market who knew nothing about the market, except they were going to make some quick money. And the thing was obviously overblown."

Gradually, a new wave of Wall Street Pigs squeezed out of their pens, infiltrating the market. These unsavory brokers pressured their investors to buy dubious stocks. Sheep investors gladly opened both ears to these investors. They fell for thinly veiled lies about how these fabricated companies were about to make it big.

Many investors began to purchase stocks on credit, which was a big no-no in the industry. In Wall Street, this was known as "buying on margin." If the investor was considered a good customer, they were allowed to buy stocks at a 10% margin. To paint a clearer picture, this meant that by putting up just $100, an investor could own a share of a stock valued at $1,000. The remaining $900 credit would then become collateral for a loan. As the public grew increasingly comfortable with purchasing on credit, a few skeptical investors voiced their concerns. They spotted shadows of a storm brewing overhead, wondering how long these "good times" would last.

Among the skeptics were Joseph Kennedy and the once eager advocate, Groucho Marx. Kennedy sensed that something was not sitting right with the market. He wrote in his memoir, "If the shoe shine guy knows as much as I do about the stock market, maybe it's time for me to get out." Marx apparently contacted his broker at one point, complaining that he could not understand why prices kept going up. As a reply, the broker informed him that this was now a "global economy," and things were different, a phrase that has been uttered time and time again. Even Herbert Hoover, the President himself, began to approach his Wall Street friends, wondering if this was cause for alarm.

In 1928, Charles E. Merrill, one of the founders of the Merrill Lynch Firm, issued a daunting warning to his clients. In the letter, Merrill wrote, "Now is a good time to get out of debt. We do not urge that you sell securities indiscriminately, but we do advise, in no uncertain terms, that you should take advantage of present high prices and put your own financial house in order." It appeared that the skeptics' concerns had more validity than they thought.

In 1929, things began to get ugly. The once booming sales of "big ticket" goods tumbled, triggering the decline of multiple big-name stocks. The abrupt decline in the market prompted a nationwide margin call. The phones of investors rang off the hook with thousands of brokers on the other end of the line. Anxious brokers pestered the investors to inject more money into their stock market accounts.

People began to realize the dangers of buying stock on credit. But by then, it was too late. When the price of a stock shrinks, the dwindling worth of the stock is no longer fit to be collateral for the loan. The only way to even out the stock and loan was to push the investors to put up more margins, or scrounge up whatever cash they could give. If investors failed to do so, their accounts were liquidated.

On September 5, Roger Babson told a meeting of the National Business Conference, "I repeat what I said at this time last year and the year before, that sooner or later a crash is coming which will take in the leading stocks and cause a decline of from 60 to 80 points in the Dow-Jones Barometer. Fair weather cannot always continue. The economic cycle is in progress today as it was in the past. The Federal Reserve System has put the banks in a strong position, but it has not changed human nature. More people are borrowing and speculating today than ever in our history. Sooner or later a crash is coming and it may be terrific. Wise are those investors who now get out of debt and reef their sails. This does not mean selling all you have, but it does mean paying up your loans and avoiding margin speculation…Sooner or later the stock market boom will collapse like the Florida boom. Someday the time is coming when the market will begin to slide off, sellers will exceed buyers, and paper profits will being to disappear. Then there will immediately be a stampede to save what paper profits then exist."

Babson

Some people listened to his words and considered them more reliable than those of Evangeline Adams (who was still predicting a rise), and the market dipped in response. This was later called the Babson Break, named after Babson, and two days later, the *Chicago Tribune* reported, "Roger Babson's dire predictions of an 'inevitable crash' in the stock market, which would some time break the averages 60 to 80 points, evoked retorts today from economists, stock exchange houses, and others, most of whom took an opposite view or advised clients and the public not to be stampeded by Mr. Babson's forecast of a collapse that would rival that of the Florida land boom. Mr. Babson's view was directly controverted by Prof. Irving Fisher of Yale University, an economist of highest standing. Prof. Fisher flatly asserted that 'stock prices are not high and Wall Street will not experience anything in the nature of a crash.'"

Over the next few weeks, prices continued to go up and down. Reuban Cain, a stock salesman at the time, later recalled, "I remember well that I thought, 'Why is this doing this?' And then I thought, 'Well, I'm new here and these people' — like every day in the paper, Charlie Mitchell would have something to say, the J.P. Morgan people would have something to say about how good things were — and I thought, 'Well, they know a lot more about this market than I do. I'm fairly new here and I really can't see why it's going up.' But then, when they say it can't go down or if it does go down today, it'll go back tomorrow, you think, 'Well, they really are like God. They know it all and it must be the way it's going because they say so.'"

Meanwhile, *The World* ran a headline on October 4 that read "Brokers to Open Offices on Ships," and the article announced, "The New York Stock Exchange decided yesterday to put to sea. It gave two brokerage houses permission to establish offices with continuous stock quotations by radio, on trans-Atlantic ships. Within a few weeks business will be following the flags of three nations across the bounding main. The American business man will be able to take a vacation in Europe without stopping for a single day his transactions at the center of speculation… What the psychological effect may be remains to be seen. Lady Luck always has been a favorite companion for diversions seekers at sea, a fact that has provided good incomes to many generations of traveling card players. Ships' pools and the 'horse races' on deck always have been popular. They may retain their popularity, but now they will be outclassed."

A few days later, Thomas Lamont, then the head of Morgan Bank, wrote to President Hoover and assured him, "The future appears brilliant. Our securities are the most desirable in the world." As Craig Mitchell later noted, "Practically every business leader in America, and banker, right around the time of 1929, was saying how wonderful things were and the economy had only one way to go and that was up."

On October 24, Wall Street collapsed. The financial pools of thousands of dazed investors were now bone-dry. None of them could hand over the required funds when it was time for their brokers to enter the exchange. At 10 AM sharp, the brass alarm reverberated across the gloomy trading floor, signaling the start of the liquidation sales. Geneen, who was also present on that fateful day, said it was just like any other busy day. But as the day went on, things only got worse. It became clear that no one was interested in buying – everyone was looking to shake off their now questionable stocks.

The usual hubbub on the trading floor morphed into panic. The holes the countrywide "credit binge" were poking had gotten so out of hand, the market quickly collapsed on itself. Stock prices continued to plummet throughout the day, which led to even more margin calls that resulted in liquidation. Desperate brokers were selling so many shares at once that the ticker was lagging on a 4-hour delay. Worried investors clogged the streets outside the entrance, demanding to know what was going on.

Out of nowhere, the Vice President of the exchange, Richard Whitney, took a brave step forward. He summoned the nation's top bankers and trotted off to the trading floor. With a puffed out chest, he purchased $20 million worth of stock, all in a matter of minutes. The public cheered, believing Whitney was here to haul them out of the slump.

Craig Mitchell described the day: "The market opened in an absolutely free fall and some people couldn't even get any bids for their shares and it was wild panic. And an ugly crowd gathered outside the stock exchange and it was described as making weird and threatening noises. It was, indeed, one of the worst days that had ever been seen down there."

Hopeful that he could do something like Charles Mitchell had done back in March, the men of Wall Street turned their eyes to Thomas Lamont, who they hoped would intervene. According to Lamont's grandson Edward, "Tom Lamont called a number of the other bankers, like Charles Mitchell of the National City Bank and people from the Bankers Trust and J. Albert Wiggin of the Chase Bank and so forth — there were about a half a dozen of them there — and they were gathered together to really discuss what they could do to stem this tremendous onslaught of selling stocks on the stock exchange that was taking place."

Charles Mitchell agreed to help. As his son later put it, "About 12:30, there was an announcement that this group of bankers would make available a very substantial sum to ease the credit stringency and support the market. And right after that, Dick Whitney made his famous walk across the floor of the New York Stock Exchange." Arriving at the Stock Exchange, Whitney made a very public showing of ordering 10,000 shares of U.S. Steel at a higher price than it was selling at that time. Horace Silverstone, who was there that day, explained, "He stood up on one of the seats at the post and he said, 'I give 45 for 50,000 Standard Oil,' and everybody started to applaud. 'Oh, the crash is over. If Morgan's putting his money in, then maybe the crash is over.'" Edward Lamont noted that his ancestor felt the same way: "The *New York Times* said that thanks to the formation of this bankers pool, most observers felt that the panic and the great sell-off was over. And most people did feel that way. Tom Lamont felt that way."

Nonetheless, on that Thursday, a *New York Times* headline read "Prices of Stocks Drop in Heavy Liquidation; Total Drop of Billions." According to the report, "Frightened by the decline in stock prices during the last month and a half, thousands of stockholders dumped their shares on the market yesterday afternoon in such an avalanche of selling as to bring about one of the widest declines in history. Even the best of seasoned, dividend paying shares were sold regardless of the prices they would bring, and the result was a tremendous smash in which stocks lost from a few points to as much as ninety-six."

As the next few days passed, the public grew uneasy. It seemed that they had celebrated too early, as Whitney's generosity had nothing to do with saving the market. In fact, he was looking to fool the market so banks could eventually be sold at a higher price.

Nonetheless, on Monday, margin calls compelled investors to sell off their holdings, and the Dow suffered a record loss of over 38 points, representing more than 13% overall. Galbraith explained the events of the day: "Monday, October 28, was the first day on which this process of climax and anticlimax ad infinitum began to reveal itself. It was another terrible day. Volume was huge, although below the previous Thursday— nine and a quarter million shares as compared with nearly thirteen. But the losses were far more severe. The Times industrials were down 49 points for the day. General Electric was off 48; Westinghouse, 34; Tel and Tel, 34. Steel went down 18 points. Indeed, the decline on this one day was greater than that of all the preceding week of panic. Once again a late ticker left everyone in ignorance of what was happening, save that it was bad. On this day there was no recovery. At one-ten Charles E. Mitchell was observed going into Morgan's, and the news ticker carried the magic word. Steel rallied and went from 194 to 198. But Richard Whitney did not materialize. It seems probable in light of later knowledge that Mitchell was on the way to float a personal loan. The market weakened again, and in the last hour a phenomenal three million shares— a big day's business before and ever since— changed hands at rapidly falling prices."

Reporter Jonathan Leonard described the scene in the wake of October 28: "That night Wall Street was lit up like a Christmas tree. Restaurants, barber shops, and speakeasies were open and doing a roaring business. Messenger boys and runners raced through the streets whooping and singing at the tops of their lungs. Slum children invaded the district to play with balls of ticker tape. Well-dressed gentlemen fell asleep in lunch counters. All the downtown hotels, rooming houses, even flophouses were full of financial employees who usually slept in the Bronx. It was probably Wall Street's worst night. Not only had the day been bad, but everybody down to the youngest office boy had a pretty good idea of what was going to happen tomorrow."

It would be known as "Black Monday," but the trouble was far from over. Tuesday, October 29, dawned cold and dreary in New York as the stock market opened to what soon became a disaster. As the day continued, it was clear that panicked investors were doing everything they could to pull out of the market, and by the end of the day, the Dow had lost another 12% of its value overall.

At 9:20 a.m. that morning, Lawrence Richey, President Hoover's secretary, telegraphed him: "Mr. President: – Mr. Rand, of Remington-Rand Company New York has just telephoned stating that he thinks you should issue statement to the press tonight for publication tomorrow morning, such as this:— 'I am of the opinion that speculators excessives have been thoroughly liquidated [sold] and sound investment securities [stocks and bonds] have been reduced to a safe and attractive [price] level. Now is the time for Bankers, Brokers, and Investors to exercise the utmost of patience and cool judgment in all dealings with one another.' Mr. Rand states that conditions are very serious and if exist for day or two longer as they have for past few days, will result in ruining millions of business people. States reaction not alone in New York, but all over the Country, as he has been in touch with different sections of the country over long-distance phone, and states business people of the Country are looking to you for some such statement to save the situation."

The World's optimistic headline read "Gigantic Bank Pool Pledged To Avert Disaster as Second Big Crash Stuns Wall Street Largest Financial Powers in the City Meet After Day of Hysterical Liquidation Sinking Prices Below Thursday's." The article reported, "After the stock market had come crashing down again in a veritable deluge of forced and hysterical liquidation, word sped through the financial district last evening that the largest banks in the city were prepared to exert their organized power this morning to prevent further disaster. Arrangements described as "fully adequate" were completed at a conference at the offices of J. P. Morgan & Co. at Broad and Wall Streets... Although no formal statement was issued, it was the consensus of those at the meeting that the worst of the liquidation is over and that a natural demand for investment stocks now available on the bargain counter should go far toward an immediate restoration of trading stability."

Obviously that did not work, and the next day the *New York Evening Post* reported, "It is clear that the Street is going through the greatest disaster in its history. No fair words can gloss over that fact. Because there is no tightness of money we are without the most familiar feature of a bad [economic] time. Furthermore, the stock market has been operating so independently of business that we have not yet realized the larger results of its break. Nevertheless, good must come even from this stern and cruel housecleaning. The country will go back to work…That means here, as it meant in postwar Germany, a revival of values. How can any cool head fail to agree with Professor Irving Fisher's declaration that standard American stocks have gone so much too low as to be crying to be bought? Such stocks are the bone and sinew of the country. Not to believe in them is not to believe in America. The world has so many things that must be done, and no one can do them better than our own people. Our business strength has pulled us out of difficulties in days gone by. With faith it will do it again."

By the end of the week, General Electric, which was once valued at $1,612 per share, dropped to $154. Automobile giant General Motors went from $1,075 each to a measly $40. The Dow-Jones Industrial Average shot down 89%. Perhaps the most sobering statistic of all, over $72 billion of investments were flushed down the drain. Those that had bet their entire life savings on these investments were beside themselves, seeing countless families ruined.

Groucho Marx was unable to escape the wrath of the depression. He was said to have been emotionally traumatized by the crash, slipping into a "lifelong struggle with insomnia." Still, despite the loss of his life savings, Marx was considered one of the lucky ones. He was in a profession that allowed him to continue to earn a living throughout the years of the depression. Arthur Marx recalled, "My father was ready to kill himself. In the morning of the crash, he got a call and it was Max Gordon and Max Gordon says, 'Groucho?' and my father said, 'What?' And Gordon said, 'Groucho, the jig is up.'"

Reuben Cain, who had been a stock salesman up until the time of the crash, said, 'There were all sorts of rumors and you'd see people going down the street looking up to see if they could catch somebody jumping out the window. Now, it turned out there weren't as many people who jumped out the window as they reported, but some did and others committed suicide other ways."

Rita Cushman later remembered, "This house was taken over, of course, and things changed. And I began to know what the real world was all about. It was about time. I was 19 years old." Her father ended October 1929 with $12 million in debt but paid off what he owed and lived long enough to die in 1955 as a respected member of Wall Street.

One historian described the instantaneous effects it had elsewhere: "Five hundred miles from Wall Street in the Atlantic, the luxury liner, the Berengaria, was heading home. From Michael Meehan's brokerage office, word spread through the ship: 'The bottom's fallen out of the market.' Men came running out of their Turkish baths in towels. Card games ended abruptly. Everyone tried to jam into the tiny office, yelling, 'Sell at market!' They had left England wealthy men. They docked in New York without a penny."

On a side note, one of the most interesting myths about Wall Street is tied to this crash. As the myth goes, ruined brokers were throwing themselves out of windows in droves. Allegedly, clerks in hotels were asking customers whether they wanted a room for sleeping or jumping upon checking in. The reality was this was merely an example of the media spinning stories out of control. After the 1929 crash, there were over 100 documented suicides, and only 4 were linked to the crash. However, it appeared more people resorted to self-immolation, self-inflicted gunshots, gassing, and jumping from bridges as suicide methods.

This downward spiral carried on for the following 3 years. For a full decade, the United States felt the burn of one what experts call the "worst economic collapse in the history of the modern industrial world." While the public sunk deeper into the Great Depression, they grew hostile towards Wall Street. They blamed the smooth-talking members of Wall Street for causing the crash.

There was no doubt about it – something had to be done.

A Time for Change

"After the collapse of Wall Street in the 1920s, the culture stopped being all about the money, and the country survived and ultimately flourished." – Graydon Carter, *Vanity Fair* editor

In 1932, the United States welcomed Franklin Roosevelt as the country's 32nd president, and his very first speech to the public was a firm message that called for immediate change. He targeted the stock market as his first call for reform. Standing behind a podium before thousands of spectators, he announced, "There must be strict supervision of all banking, and credit, and investment. There must be an end to speculation of other people's money." With every breath between each proclamation, the crowd received him with raucous applause.

When President Roosevelt stepped into office in 1933, he went to work immediately. On the second day of his presidency, he ordered the New York stock exchange offices to close for a week. Then, he tackled Congress, ticking off a list of reforms that were to be put into action as soon as possible.

First, banks were no longer allowed to "gamble" on stocks. The tarnished reputation of stock brokers was to end right then. Brokers were now expected to treat their customers' money as if it were their own. If corporations wished to resume offering stocks to the public, they had to file detailed financial reports with a government agency every year. With the ability to gain access to clearer information, as well as the tighter and more regulated system set in place, the public's confidence in stock investment was restored.

At this stage, Richard Whitney had been promoted to President of the stock exchange. As to be expected, he was less than pleased with President Roosevelt's sweeping reforms. He appeared on live television, speaking ill of the new regulations and stating that Wall Street was fully equipped to handle matters on their own. In plainer terms, he wanted the government to stay out of Wall Street.

In spite of Whitney's televised threats, President Roosevelt was not fazed. It only fired up his drive for government control over Whitney's precious Wall Street. On June 6, 1934, he founded the Securities and Exchange Commission (SEC) with the sole task of enforcing these rules. Joseph Kennedy was assigned as the SEC's first chairman.

The SEC indicted an alarming number of over 300 people. The Pigs and Wolves of Wall Street either retreated into the shadows or were forced to change their ways, hoping to evade the patrolling eyes of the SEC. Even with the indictments, the SEC had trouble making any of the convictions stick, but many felt deep satisfaction when the only major figure to ever be convicted was none other than Whitney. He was charged with embezzlement and carted off to the notorious Sing Sing Prison, where he spent a total of 3 years.

Regardless of President Roosevelt's new regulations, the Wall Street craze fizzled. The people lost their ravenous hunger for paper exchange, and brokers quit in droves, leaving in search for concrete jobs with a steadier paycheck.

Unlike the First World War, the federal government funded the effort to jumpstart the economy after World War II. The stock market was only responsible for 20%. Though Wall Street had seen better years financially, the end of the war in September of 1945 gifted them with a positive turning point.

Before this, women were only allowed in the back rooms of the Wall Street offices. They were limited to jobs with lighter responsibilities such as clerks and stenographers. In 1945, the first batch of female stock brokers joined the men on the trading floor. Dressed in classy collared dresses fitted with shoulder pads, the women marched onto the floor, ready to make a name for themselves.

The years that followed the war were prosperous, running on the nation's refreshed ambition – the Baby Boom years. Once again, the public warmed up to the idea of stock investment. Investors learned from the mistakes of those that had lost everything in the 1929 crash. They were now wiser, making calculated decisions as opposed to speculating.

Charles Merrill took advantage of the steadily growing economy and seized his opportunity. He opened up hundreds of new Merrill Lynch offices in the suburbs. This was an insightful move on his part, tweaking the damaged reputation of Wall Street stock brokers. Next, Merrill put out several ads on the papers, listing the qualities of his ideal candidates. The ad read, "The person we're after is a GI, ex-GI, with a wife, 3 kids, and a Chevy." It appeared as if an average, middle class citizen had a real shot at making it big in the business someday.

The women of the community were not forgotten. Merrill set up a series of investment classes for women, all of which he personally taught. An empty seat in these classes was a rarity. Later, Merrill erected a pop-up "How to Invest" exhibit in New York's Grand Central Station. The exhibit featured multiple television screens propped up on all 4 sides, along with Merrill Lynch employees beyond tables handing out information pamphlets and research booklets for free.

Another significant innovation that would take Wall Street and the public by storm came with economist Harry Markowitz from the University of Chicago. In 1952, he published an essay focusing on what he called the "Modern Portfolio Theory." In the industry, it is better known as "stock diversification." Markowitz encouraged investors all over the country to purchase a wide range of stocks from different fields. This, he believed, would boost one's chances against bankruptcy if one stock were to fail. Eventually, this radical idea earned Markowitz a Nobel Prize for Economics, and today, many investors still play by Markowitz's golden rule.

The Broadway Boom

"The show must go on…I have found: action, camera, and sound…where the flowers don't smell and the fruit has no taste; where everyone's nearly as stupid as I, but oh so very few can get a break and can die." – "Miss Day," Bruz Fletcher

The early 1920s saw the advent of yet another indispensable constituent to modern Broadway – the LGBT community. When the United States was thrust into the Prohibition Era, a country-wide ban on the manufacture, transportation, and sale of alcohol, the nation slipped into what is now referred to as the "Pansy Craze." While bootleggers were busy slinging unmarked barrels of liquor from one hideout to another, the gay nightclub scene burst forth and prospered. These nightclubs were no longer confined to Harlem, but began to mingle with mainstream culture and branch out to big cities such as San Francisco, Los Angeles, and Manhattan.

Gay, lesbian, transgendered, and cross-dressing performers unlocked their closets and marched onto the stages of every venue imaginable, and became instant icons. No stage was too small for such a transformative period in history. Even newspapers, such as the Pittsburgh Courier and the Baltimore African American, printed issues with sultry and delightful drag queens splashed across the front page. Even the most "reputable" establishments hosted exotic balls, fabulous concerts, and beauty contests for drag kings and queens.

Swarms, sometimes in the thousands, gathered to see the gay performers, branded "pansies," and lesbian artists, otherwise known as "bull-dikers," in the flesh. One of the greatest drag queens of the era was Ray (or Rae) Bourbon, who delighted audiences with his scandalous monologues and edgy stand-up comedy routines. In 1944, Mae West, a known LGBT rights advocate, cast Bourbon as "Florian" in her Broadway show, Catherine Was Great.

Sadly, when Prohibition ended in 1932, the Pansy Craze petered out almost as quickly as it came. The authorities implemented draconian laws in an attempt to suffocate the rainbow community, such as New York's 1927 "padlock bill," which outright banned all LGBT matters from the Broadway stage, and the Hays Code of 1934, which did the same for the big screen. The public opinion of the LGBT community reverted to its narrow-minded ways, and sneering audiences were no longer laughing with the bold performers, but at them. One such name who was especially traumatized by the abrupt shift was Bruz Fletcher, a singer from Los Angeles with a uniquely pleasant, youthful tone to his voice. Unable to find steady employment, Fletcher spiraled into a horrible depression, and ultimately took his own life.

It would take another 4 decades before the LGBT community made its long-awaited return with Mart Crowley's 1964 production of The Boys in the Band, which went on to run for 1,001 shows.

In 1982, the Andrew Lloyd Weber and Cameron Mackintosh original, Cats, captivated a worldwide audience, and in effect, "reinvigorated" the Broadway interest among the masses. This whimsical musical based on a band of limber, soul-searching cats in skin-tight and brightly-colored leotards sold out season after season, amounting to 7,845 performances in its lifetime. It became the longest-running Broadway musical until it was upstaged by another Weber original, The Phantom of the Opera, which has staged more than 12,000 shows in over 3 decades and counting, crossing the seas to 166 cities in 35 countries, with an audience reach of over 140 million.

The 21st century saw the surfacing of another ingenious mind that brought Broadway to a level unseen nor heard of before. On July 13, 2015, Lin-Manuel Miranda, gifted the world with the

Grammy-winning Hamilton, a historic and historical musical about Alexander Hamilton. Miranda's creative and sophisticated use of hip-hop, razor-sharp lyrics, and clever casting has made it an impossible phenomenon to miss in this day and age.

Major celebrities and politicians alike have been elbowing each other out of the way to the front of the queue, but even they have found it a mission to score tickets. By February of 2016, the show had cashed in $82 million on "in advance" ticket sales. Even more dizzying a fact is its $500,000 in weekly profits, which is only paled by forecasts from experts that estimate that Hamilton is on course to rake in $1 billion from New York alone. Another critically acclaimed behemoth of the 21st century is the Book of Mormon, created by playwrights Matt Stone and Trey Parker of South Park fame. In 2013, Forbes announced that it took home an average of $19 million a month.

Though plenty of critics today might claim that Broadway is the most diverse it has ever been – which is technically true in a world that is only black-and-white – Asian American actors and thespians from other minorities, still struggle to squeeze their way into the limelight. As recently as October of 2016, there were only 3 Asian American leads on Broadway – 2 in Alaadin, and Ali Ewoldt as the first Asian Christine in The Phantom of the Opera. Ruthie Ann Miles, the first Asian American to bag a Tony award for her role in the King and I, was not given this honor until 2015. At that point, only 5 Asian Americans in all of history had ever won such a distinction, but 28 white Americans had succeeded in taking home a trophy for Asian productions. Miles commented of the unfortunate reality: "Diversity is not just black and white...There are such massive groups of people that are just completely missing from the equation."

That being the case, lovers of Broadway are optimistic that change will continue to remain a constant on the Great White Way.

The Age of Computers

"Technology...is a queer thing. It brings you great gifts with one hand, and it stabs you in the back with the other." – C.P. Snow

As the United States transitioned to the 1960s and 1970s, the market saw its fair share of bad days. Yet another disaster was about to strike, but this was one that was unlike any other. Wall Street had unwillingly entered what many refer to today as the 1960s Paperwork Panic.

There were now more brokers on the trading floor than ever. Plus, with the rising figures of mutual funds and pension plans, trading volume was now at a staggering 11 million shares a day. The problem was, these 11 million trades were implemented by hand. Clerks clocked out each day with a strained back and gelatin legs from being hunched over and on their feet all day. Most were suffering from paper cuts and cases of "trigger finger," kneading their misshapen fingers caused by hours of vigorous scribbling. During working hours, mountains of stacked papers were a common sight on the clerks' desks. Naturally, the increasing volume of paperwork led to delays. Every week, barely lucid clerks were unable to finish their paperwork in time. The problem became so dire that the stock exchange at New York began closing their doors on Wednesdays so the clerks could catch up on their work. Cots started to pop up all over the offices. Clerks were so exhausted from working around the clock that they worked out shifts. While the others worked, 1 or 2 were allowed to duck out of the room for a quick snooze on the cots. With some of the worst cases, clerks would not leave the office for weeks.

The clerks' exhaustion was one matter, but many began to abuse the delirium on the trading floor from the endless paper-crunching. There were common mix-ups from communication errors. These prompted failed trades, brokerages, and market shutdowns. And then there were those that took the chance to milk the system. A *New York Times* article that researched Wall Street's activities from 1967-1970 reported that there were over $400 million in stolen securities. Today, that is a figure equivalent to $2.8 billion. The same article reported that one 22-year-old broker was charged with stealing over $900,000 in IBM stock certificates.

Perhaps the gravest setback of all was the cash flow chaos that ensued. The crisis was at its height in 1968. In a few months' time, nearly 100 companies filed for bankruptcy.

In addition to the complications from the Vietnam War, politically charged issues from the Kennedy to Carter years contributed to market upsets. One of these major events was the OPEC Oil Crisis of 1973. The members of the Organization of Arab Petroleum Exporting Companies ceased oil trade with Japan, Canada, the Netherlands, the United Kingdom, and the United States. A year after the ban, the price per barrel had shot up from $3 to $12 in the United States. Gas stations across the country were at their wit's end, scrambling to service the long lines of troubled Americans waiting for a gallon of gas.

Wall Street stumbled upon its saving grace with yet another striking technological advance – computers. In the 1970s, Wall Street replaced their antiquated ticker machines and paper-pushing system with its first electronic system. Now, smaller transactions were sent straight to their assigned trading posts. Clerks were finally relieved of the draining handwritten task, and computers were now programmed to handle the quickly swelling volume of trades.

The National Association of Securities Dealers Automated Quotations, or NASDAQ, was founded by the NASD in 1971. In February of 1971, they began trading as the world's first ever electronic stock market. Stock trading was now based on a computerized bulletin board system, as well as over the phone. NASDAQ provided an inexpensive way to trade, cutting corners to render face-to-face encounters obsolete. Brokerage houses were now linked around the globe.

By the 1980s, Wall Street had become completely reliant on the new computerized system, and little did anyone know, this exact entity was about to betray them. On October 19, 1987, Wall

Street was hit with another wave of déjà vu. The market was failing – and fast.

Computers were still running on what many today consider an archaic system. They were pre-programmed to automatically sell stocks when prices reached a certain number. One simple press of a button and the stock was sold. This created a chain reaction, setting off one computer after another. With trading volumes higher than ever, it was a fiasco even all the clerks in Wall Street put together could not contain. The Dow-Jones Average sunk 508 points, losing 22.6% of its value. This translated to a ground-quaking loss of over $500 billion. October 19th of 1987 is now glumly remembered as "Black Monday," one of the largest one-day crashes in all of Wall Street history.

Black Monday was a brutal day for Wall Street, but like other disasters, experts learned from it. The NYSE revamped the computers with a circuit-breaker program. This program fixed the bug, restricting trading in the case of unsteady DOW fluctuations.

The 2008 Housing Fiasco

"Many of us like to think of financial economics as a science, but complex events like the financial crisis suggest that this conceit may be more wishful thinking than reality." – Andrew Lo, MIT professor

On December 15, 1989, enthusiastic crowds on Broad Street assembled outside the NYSE building. A 7,000 lb sculpture of a handsome bull was sitting under a towering Christmas tree. Earlier that morning, Sicilian artist Arturo DiModica snuck onto Broad Street with his masterpiece. Having timed the schedule of the roaming security, he dropped the bull off under the tree and went on his merry way. This was DiModica's gift to the American public. Standing at 11 feet, with an imposing 18 foot long torso, the "Charging Bull" symbolized "the power of the American people." Intentionally installed just 2 years after Black Monday, DiModica wanted to reinvigorate the people's spirit, bringing light to their unyielding determination and the better days coming ahead.

Since no one had ordered the statue, Wall Street authorities got rid of it the same day. The move made the *New York Post* headlines the next morning: "Bah, Humbug! New York Stock Exchange Grinches Can't Bear Christmas Gift Bull." The City of New York graciously accepted the gift instead, and the "Charging Bull," a.k.a the "Wall Street Bull," is now permanently residing in Bowling Green Park.

The decades that followed saw a few hiccups in the market, but all in all, Wall Street sailed to the 2000s. During 9/11, Wall Street suffered some of the damage, including physically. The *New York Times* reported, "Debris littered some streets of the financial district. National Guard members in camouflage uniforms manned checkpoints. Abandoned coffee carts, glazed with dust from the collapse of the World Trade Center, lay on their sides across sidewalks. Most subway stations were closed, most lights were still off, most telephones did not work, and only a handful of people walked in the narrow canyons of Wall Street yesterday morning." It was estimated that a substantial portion of Wall Street's office space was hopelessly ruined.

In 2008, Wall Street witnessed a catastrophe that would not only affect the United States but billions around the world. On September 29, 2008, the Dow-Jones Average took a hurtling nosedive of 777.68 points. The ghastly crash came after Congressmen rejected a $700 billion bailout bill.

How did it come to this? The start of 2007 seemed to be a promising year. The Dow-Jones Average was closing at a glowing figure of approximately 12,460. Coming a long way from its early years, the Average had grown from observing 12 to the 30 most significant stocks trading on the NYSE and NASDAQ. As months passed, the Average continued to scale new heights. October 2007 saw the Average at an all-time high: 14,164.43.

Still, some were disturbed by the climbing Average. Chin-stroking skeptics, who had noticed the slowdown of the turbulent housing market, began to raise red flags. Some of these skeptics had already begun to smell fish the year prior. The most memorable of these red flags was the warning issued by The Commerce Department in November of 2006. For the month of October, the number of new home permits was 28% lower than it had been in October of 2005. The housing market suffered a huge plunge in prices in 2006, inevitably leading to defaults on sub-prime mortgages.

The mortgage was a phenomenon invented by insurance companies in the 1930s. To buy a house, many families turned to these insurance companies for substantial loans. In exchange, they received a piece of paper called a "mortgage." Every month, homeowners were expected to pay back portions of the loan attached with interest rates. Failed payments granted these insurance companies or banks the right to confiscate the homeowner's properties.

Authorities soon realized that the mortgage payment system was detrimental to the average family. Over a period of 3-5 years, mortgage loan terms were limited to 50% of the house's market value, and the payment ended with a balloon sum. In 1934, the Federal Housing Administration established the modern mortgage still used today, enforcing new regulations with banks across the nation. A new, stricter program was aimed at those who were not eligible for the previous programs.

Today, mortgages operate in a similar fashion. If a homeowner was to stop paying their mortgage, they would have to default. The mortgage is often passed on from one bank or company to another. Those with their hands on the mortgage are then granted ownership of the house. It is very common for banks to sell mortgages to third parties.

Back then, banks were only interested in candidates that could give proof of steady income and above-average credit, but in the 2000s, this attitude began to change. The market saw an alarming increase of sub-prime mortgages, which were loans given to potential homeowners with poor credit ratings who did not qualify for traditional mortgages. To level out the risk, the bank or company slapped on a higher interest rate.

For the first years of the new millennium, investors began pouring their money into the housing market. By doing so, the investors hoped to plump up their cash cows with profits from the interest rates that homeowners paid on their mortgages. Once trusted bonds like the U.S. Treasury were now losing its luster, paying what the investors considered to be scant interest rates, so fat-cat global investors began purchasing mortgage-backed securities. This is when financial institutions "securitize" mortgages. Securitizing is when assets that are not easily converted to cash are turned into securities. The investors indulged themselves with a shopping spree of thousands of individual mortgages. They then balled up these mortgages in one pool and sold shares of it to other investors. Across the country, thousands of investors competed for a dip in that pool.

From the exterior, these shares seemed like perfectly safe bets. After all, the housing market was apparently on the rise. Investors believed that if worst came to worst and borrowers defaulted on their mortgages, the house would simply be sold for more money. Even credit ratings agencies promoted the idea of mortgage-backed securities to their customers as secure investments. These agencies went so far as to award the securities with "AAA" ratings.

Investors were desperate to quench their now intensifying thirst for mortgage-backed securities. Lenders needed to figure out a way to fulfill that demand. To do so, they needed more mortgages, so banks and companies across the nations lowered their standards, granting more sub-prime mortgages than they ever had. They targeted humble households with poor credit ratings and low income. This was already a practice that was frowned upon in the industry, but slippery institutions started getting greedy.

These institutions began utilizing tactics called "predatory lending practices" to create mortgages. They passed out loans carelessly without conducting background checks or verifying income. The adjustable rate mortgages offered by these companies were tricky and unfairly sugarcoated. These were payments people could afford initially, but would grow beyond their means in no time.

Sub-prime mortgages and newfangled predatory lending practices were still unknown to the majority of the public, and these companies wanted to keep it that way. This gave them the freedom to promote mortgage debts as stellar bets. The reality was the exact opposite, but the investors' faith in ratings was solid, and they continued to fatten up this new segment of the market with their dough. An even riskier product that traders began to offer were CDOs – collateralized debt obligations.

At the same time, the increasingly lax lending requirements, along with sinking interest rates, drove up housing prices. This gave the public more reason to believe these were wise investments. As the skeptics predicted, the nation found themselves in yet another bubble.

The bubble burst. People failed to keep up with their constantly growing mortgage payments. Like dominoes, the borrowers began defaulting, giving them no choice but to put up more houses for sale. Unfortunately, buyers now had cold feet – no one was looking to buy.

Next, home prices went from fumbling to a lightning-fast tumble. Some families were now lugging around hulking mortgages way more than their homes were actually worth. Then, those borrowers who could not make the monthly bills were forced to default too, pushing housing prices down even further.

Huge financial institutions that were once on the up and up ceased all purchase of sub-prime mortgages. Sub-prime lenders were now piling up on shoddy loans. By 2007, some of the biggest lenders in the business filed for bankruptcy. The investment from investors who had injected big money into these CDOs and mortgage-backed companies virtually evaporated.

Fanning the flames was another dilemma many of these financial institutions had overlooked. Banks had been selling unregulated derivatives on the market, the most serious of which were credit default swaps. Swaps were exchanged as insurance policies for mortgage-backed securities. One of the major companies that fell prey to this was the American International Group (AIG). AIG sold billions of dollars worth of these policies without having sufficient funds to back them up in the event of an emergency.

All these problems only added to a convoluted tangle of assets, liabilities, and risks. Everything was connected, so when things went wrong, it impacted the entirety of the complex entity.

The unsettled public watched as some of the country's major companies fell into decline. The Lehman Brothers declared bankruptcy. Others followed suit, were forced to enter mergers, or had to knock on the government's door for bailouts.

As a result, in September 2008, everything came undone. Wall Street and credit markets were at a standstill, unleashing another storm of nationwide panic. That year, the United States faced another one of its worst recessions.

2008 saw a number of arrests for fraud and embezzlement, and Wall Street was in for another shock when investment adviser Bernie Madoff was hauled into police custody on December 11. After skulking under the radar for years, Madoff sent the nation gasping when he admitted to headlining a $50 billion Ponzi scheme and concealing millions of dollars in taxes from the IRS.

In the midst of the crisis, the Federal Reserve strode up to the plate, offering emergency loans to banks. This was an effort to keep reputable banks with increasingly shy lenders from collapsing. They established TARP, the Troubled Assets Relief Program, a bank bailout. $250 billion was spent to bail out these institutions, and would later help General Motors, AIG, and homeowners get back on their feet.

Government intervention to revive the economy eventually proved at least partially effective, but the burst bubble had done its damage. CNN declared the following year the "Worst Year for Jobs Since '45" in one of its headlines, and 2008 alone saw the axing of 2.6 million jobs, equivalent to the total number of jobs there are in states like Maryland, Missouri, and Wisconsin. By 2010, that figure had grown by 5.3 million, and this was only in the United States.

In 2014, a *Los Angeles Times* article celebrated a milestone for the American economy. Though change had been sluggish, the economy had reportedly recovered the millions of jobs lost since the 2008 crash. That said, a 2015 report by the International Labor Organization highlighted the 61 million jobs lost across the world since the 2008 recession, and Director-General Guy Ryder shared his concerns with the global economy. Though the economy in Japan and the United States are on the path to recovery, a number of advanced economies, most notably in Europe, have yet to find their way. Ryder ended his statement by noting, "This means the job crisis is far from over so there is no place for complacency."

Once again, Wall Street's credibility has been put to question by the American public. The Occupy Together movement, a self-proclaimed leaderless organization, took matters into their own hands on September 17, 2011. Through Facebook, Twitter, and other social media mediums, the movement called for an event they named "Occupy Wall Street." Peaceful protesters branched out over the 8 blocks of Wall Street with the Charging Bull as their home base. The crowd was colorful and varied, coming with marching bands and impromptu yoga and Tai Chi classes at the Bowling Green Park to add to the fiery atmosphere.

The protesters rallied for justice against social and economical injustice around the world. Many wanted "corrupt" leaders from financial sectors thrown behind bars. A protester expressed the group's sentiments to a CNN reporter: "Something needs to change. We need an economy for the people and by the people, not for the rich and by the rich."

The movement went viral, with many catching on to the trend, including President Obama, celebrities, and even a nod from the cyberactivist group Anonymous. Pizza joints around the country were adding cleverly named "OccuPie" flavors to their menus, and even "Occupy" video games were released.

It was clear – the people wanted change, and they wanted it now.

Wall Street Bigwigs

"Intelligence without ambition is a bird without wings." – Salvador Dali

Throughout Wall Street's multiple rises and falls, several figures have managed to shove past their counterparts to head the rat race. These key figures have risen to the top at one point in their lives through unmatched ambition and a thirst for success. Some are considered pioneers, and others despicable, but these Wall Street players have made a memorable imprint in the ongoing course of Wall Street's history.

To start off, there was John Pierpont Morgan of JPMorgan Chase Banks. It is a name that rings familiar to many, as it remains one of the largest financial institutions today. In his time, Morgan, the son of a distinguished banker, was the most powerful man on Wall Street. Under his leadership, he merged hundreds of independent factories and railroads to monopolies. But the greatest of his accomplishments came in 1901, when he combined 9 of the most prominent companies to form U.S. Steel. U.S. Steel went on to become the world's first billion-dollar corporation, and was so valuable it kicked up the Dow-Jones Average by 500%. Those around him hailed him as the "King of Corporate Mergers."

J.P. Morgan

Jay Gould was another constantly whispered name in 19th century Wall Street. Only Gould, a

Wall Street Bear, was a name that wrinkled the noses of many, often disgraced as the "Mephistopheles," or the "Devil of Wall Street." Gould was a manipulator, a pundit of the "short sale." This technique involved persuading investors to loan him their shares at a small rate of interest. With the shares in hand, he sold them at the exchange immediately. He would then drag the company's name through the mud, circulating fake rumors through the newspaper he owned. Then, he would buy back the shares at the lowest price possible and return them to the investors, raking in the profits from the difference between selling the spoiled shares and buying them back.

Gould

A modern Wall Street bad boy came in the form of Jordan Belfort. Belfort started his own investment firm, Stratton Oakmont in the 1990s. Together with his partner, Danny Porush, the Quaalude connoisseur swindled millions of dollars from his investors through a pump-and-dump scheme. His brokers thrust flimsy stocks at their clients, which led to stock price inflation. Stratton Oakmont would then dump these stocks, sell off their holdings, and dive head-first into their pool of profits. Belfort was eventually caught, sentenced to 4 years prison, and was personally fined $110 million. His lavish lifestyle of debauchery was captured in the 2013 film *The Wolf of Wall Street*, portrayed by Leonardo Di Caprio.

Jeremiah G. Hamilton was not only one of the very first African-American stock brokers, he is remembered as Wall Street's first black millionaire. At a time when racial prejudice was the norm, his business practices were considered controversial on both sides, as blacks were only expected to do business with other blacks. While he was disliked by many in the industry, he was incessantly made to face the racists that made up most of Wall Street, and he was almost lynched on more than one occasion. At the end of the day, Hamilton had the last laugh. By the time of his death in 1875, he had amassed a fortune of over $2 million ($250 million today), and was declared the richest black man in the United States.

The women of Wall Street, another formerly ignored community, worked tirelessly to climb the ranks. To begin with, there was Abigail Adams. The wife of President John Adams was the earliest documented female investor in the country. President Adams tasked his wife with overseeing the family's farm and finances as he catered to the Revolutionary War. In 1783, Abigail displayed her astute investment tactics when her husband advised her to invest in farmland. Instead, she chose to place her bets on government bonds, which brought her more returns than her husband had even imagined.

Victoria Woodhull and her sister, Tennessee Clafin, were the first women to open their own brokerage firm on Wall Street in 1970. Before that, Woodhull became the first female presidential candidate in 1872. Living in the predominantly male world of Wall Street, the sisters wore custom dress suits to take away from their femininity.

Woodhull

There was also Hetty Green, known today as the "Witch of Wall Street." Green had been under Wall Street's spell ever since she was a child, reading the financial newspaper to her father every morning. Upon her father's death, she inherited an immense fortune, and was one of the few women who had the privilege of managing their own money at the time. By investing in railroads, she quickly became the world's richest woman. In 1898, she even loaned the city of New York $1 million when they were nearing bankruptcy. Despite her riches, she was known for her cheap, crabby composure, and her refusal to let go of her wardrobe of witchy, shabby dresses. At the end of her career, Green was worth a cool $100 million.

In December 1967, Mickie Siebert of Muriel Siebert & Co. became the first woman to purchase a seat on the NYSE. The spunky Siebert was turned down by 9 potential sponsors before finally getting hold of the 2 needed to submit her application. Women across the nation saluted Siebert for breaking down yet another wall for American women.

To complete the list of firsts, there is also Suzanne Shank, the first African-American woman to run a publicly traded financial powerhouse. Shank juggles 2 major responsibilities as the CEO of Siebert Brandford Shank & Co., and in September 2015, Shank also became acting CEO of the Siebert Financial Corporation.

Conclusion

"Money is power, and you ought to be reasonably ambitious to have it." – Russell Conwell, minister and philanthropist

Wall Street continues to be a prevalent topic of public discussion today, and is one of the most debated subjects between presidential candidates. The amount of research, books, movies, and other creative works the legendary 8 blocks has spawned is in the millions, and that number is still growing. Its history is rife with controversy, complexity, and at times, chaos, but Wall Street continues to remain intrinsic to the global economy, and everyone working there knows it.

There are those who continue to defend it, praising its status for creating what they believe to be the country's most aspirant and intelligent men and women. The adrenaline one gets from the eternal chase on Wall Street is something many breathe for, excelling in a world that necessitates numbers, logic, and rational decisions. Others have labeled those in Wall Street as professional con artists, going by the old saying: "What's good for Wall Street is bad for Main Street." And who can blame them when the current top dogs are making more in one year's salary than the entire GDP of some small nations combined? In 2015, Ken Griffin, founder and CEO of Citadel, made a cheek-slapping $1.7 billion.

The reputation of Wall Street was blemished even more when a study from Canadian forensic psychologist, Robert Hare, came to light in 2012. According to his findings, 1% of the general population is psychopathic, or exhibits tendencies. 10% of that population works in financial industries.

One thing is certain. In spite of its public perception, Wall Street's contentious legacy is a force the world cannot ignore.

Online Resources

Other books about NYC history by Charles River Editors

Other books about Broadway on Amazon

Bibliography

Editors, History World. "HISTORY OF THEATRE ." *History World*. History World, 2016. Web. 31 May 2017. <http://www.historyworld.net/wrldhis/PlainTextHistories.asp?ParagraphID=cui>.

Spacey, John. "6 Types of Japanese Theatre." *Japan Talk*. Japan Talk, LLC, 3 Sept. 2015. Web. 31 May 2017. <http://www.japan-talk.com/jt/new/japanese-theatre>.

Spacey, John. "Kabuki: Welcome To The Bizarre." *Japan Talk*. Japan Talk, LLC, 20 Mar. 2015. Web. 31 May 2017. <http://www.japan-talk.com/jt/new/kabuki>.

Editors, Asian Traditional Theater and Dance. "The Early History of Chinese Theatre." *Asian Traditional Theater and Dance*. XIP, Ltd., 2010. Web. 31 May 2017. <http://www.xip.fi/atd/china/the-early-history-of-chinese-theatre.html>.

Price, Victoria, PhD. "Break a leg: A history of British theatre." *BBC iWonder*. BBC, 2015. Web. 31 May 2017. <http://www.bbc.co.uk/timelines/zwx9j6f>.

Editors, History of York. "The Mystery Plays." *History of York*. York Museums Trust , 2015. Web. 31 May 2017. <http://www.historyofyork.org.uk/themes/medieval/the-mystery-plays>.

Editors, Victoria and Albert Museum. "Elizabethan Theatre." *Victoria and Albert Museum*. Victoria and Albert Museum, London, 2016. Web. 31 May 2017. <http://www.vam.ac.uk/content/articles/e/elizabethan-theatre/>.

Editors, Shalt. "THEATRE, 1576-98." *Shakespearean London Theatre*. DeMont Fort University, Leicester, 2013. Web. 31 May 2017. <http://shalt.dmu.ac.uk/locations/theatre-1576-98.html>.

Mabillard, Amanda. "The Great Theatre." *Shakespeare Online*. Amanda Mabillard, 2010. Web. 31 May 2017. <http://www.shakespeare-online.com/theatre/burbagetheatre.html>.

Morris, Sylvia. "Shakespeare and the first actresses." *The Shakespeare Blog*. WordPress, 21 Nov. 2011. Web. 31 May 2017. <http://theshakespeareblog.com/2011/11/shakespeare-and-the-first-actresses/>.

O'Neill, Therese. "7 Games People Played in Colonial America." *Mental Floss*. Mental Floss, Inc., 2016. Web. 31 May 2017. <http://mentalfloss.com/article/51363/7-games-people-played-colonial-america>.

Geist, Christopher. "The Emergence of Popular Culture in Colonial America." *Colonial Williamsburg: That the Future May Learn from the Past.* The Colonial Williamsburg Foundation, Autumn 2006. Web. 31 May 2017. <http://www.history.org/foundation/journal/spring08/pop.cfm>.

Editors, Life in Colonial America. "Leisure." *Life in Colonial America.* Google Sites, 2013. Web. 31 May 2017. <https://sites.google.com/site/borgeslifeincolonialamerica/leisure>.

Editors, Jamestown Rediscovery. "Entertainment." *Jamestown Rediscovery.* Howell Creative Group, 2017. Web. 31 May 2017. <http://historicjamestowne.org/collections/selected-artifacts/entertainment-2/>.

Editors, Jamestown Rediscovery. "Toy House." *Colonial Williamsburg: That the Future May Learn from the Past.* The Colonial Williamsburg Foundation, 2017. Web. 31 May 2017. <http://historicjamestowne.org/selected-artifacts/toy-house/>.

Hakluyt, Richard. "Settlement and Economic Development: The Colonies to 1763 (Overview)." *Encyclopedia.Com.* The Gale Group, Inc., 2002. Web. 31 May 2017. <http://www.encyclopedia.com/history/encyclopedias-almanacs-transcripts-and-maps/settlement-and-economic-development-colonies-1763-overview>.

Editors, Boundless. "The Colonial Elite READ FEEDBACK VERSION HISTORY USAGE." *Boundless.* Boundless, Ltd., 2013. Web. 1 June 2017. <https://www.boundless.com/u-s-history/textbooks/boundless-u-s-history-textbook/expansion-of-the-colonies-1650-1750-4/social-class-in-the-colonies-54/the-colonial-elite-331-9421/>.

Editors, Jamestown Rediscovery. "Play Booth Theater." *Colonial Williamsburg: That the Future May Learn from the Past.* The Colonial Williamsburg Foundation, 2017. Web. 1 June 2017. <http://www.history.org/almanack/places/hb/hbplay.cfm>.

Stallings, Amy. "Dance during the Colonial Period." *Encyclopedia Virginia.* Virginia Foundation for the Humanities, 27 Oct. 2015. Web. 1 June 2017. <https://www.encyclopediavirginia.org/Dance_During_the_Colonial_Period#>.

Hornblow, Arthur. "THE FIRST PLAY ACTED IN NEW YORK." *Theatre History.* Theatre History, LLC, 2002. Web. 1 June 2017. <http://www.theatrehistory.com/american/hornblow02.html>.

Editors, Anthropology in Practice. "Back in Time: Walking the Wickquasgeck Trail." *Anthropology in Practice.* Blogger, 27 Nov. 2009. Web. 1 June 2017. <http://www.anthropologyinpractice.com/2009/11/back-in-time-walking-wickquasgeck-trail.html>.

Collins, Lauren. "ZOO YORK." *The New Yorker*. Conde Nast, 14 Sept. 2009. Web. 1 June 2017. <http://www.newyorker.com/magazine/2009/09/14/zoo-york>.

Editors, History Channel. "New Amsterdam becomes New York." *History Channel*. A&E Television Networks, LLC, 2015. Web. 1 June 2017. <http://www.history.com/this-day-in-history/new-amsterdam-becomes-new-york>.

Greenspan, Jesse. "The Dutch Surrender New Netherland." *History in the Headlines*. A&E Television Networks, LLC, 8 Sept. 2014. Web. 1 June 2017. <http://www.history.com/news/the-dutch-surrender-new-netherland-350-years-ago>.

Kenrick, John. "Theatre in NYC: A Brief History I." *Musicals 101*. Musicals 101, Ltd., 2005. Web. 1 June 2017. <https://www.musicals101.com/bwaythhist1.htm>.

Crews, Ed. "Drinking in Colonial America." *Colonial Williamsburg: That the Future May Learn from the Past*. The Colonial Williamsburg Foundation, 2007. Web. 1 June 2017. <http://www.history.org/foundation/journal/holiday07/drink.cfm>.

Editors, Web Books. "13. HISTORY OF COFFEE IN OLD NEW YORK." *Web Books*. Web Books, LLC, 2001. Web. 1 June 2017. <http://www.web-books.com/Classics/ON/B0/B701/18MB701.html>.

Jackson, Edwin L. "James Oglethorpe (1696-1785)." *New Georgia Encyclopedia*. University of Georgia Press, 2 Dec. 2003. Web. 1 June 2017. <http://www.georgiaencyclopedia.org/articles/government-politics/james-oglethorpe-1696-1785>.

Editors, University of Washington Libraries. "Essay: 19th Century American Theater." *University of Washington Libraries*. University of Washington Libraries, 2012. Web. 1 June 2017. <https://content.lib.washington.edu/19thcenturyactorsweb/essay.html>.

Barnett, Laura. "Musicals we love: The Beggar's Opera." *The Guardian*. Guardian News and Media, Ltd., 28 Apr. 2014. Web. 1 June 2017. <https://www.theguardian.com/stage/2014/apr/28/musicals-we-love-the-beggars-opera>.

Molnar, John W. "Theatre in Colonial Virginia." *Colonial Williamsburg: That the Future May Learn from the Past*. The Colonial Williamsburg Foundation, 2015. Web. 1 June 2017. <http://www.history.org/history/teaching/enewsletter/volume4/april06/theatre.cfm>.

Editors, History Channel. "AMERICAN REVOLUTION HISTORY." *History Channel*. A&E Television Networks, LLC, 2014. Web. 1 June 2017. <http://www.history.com/topics/american-revolution/american-revolution-history>.

Malinsky, David. "CONGRESS BANS THEATRE!" *All Things Liberty*. Journal of the American Revolution, 12 Dec. 2013. Web. 1 June 2017. <https://allthingsliberty.com/2013/12/congress-bans-theatre/>.

Cohen-Stratyner, Barbara. "British Soldiers' Theatre During the Revolutionary War." *New York Public Library*. New York Public Library, 21 Apr. 2016. Web. 1 June 2017. <https://www.nypl.org/blog/2016/04/21/british-soldiers-theatre-revolutionary-war>.

Kenrick, John. "The Black Crook (1866)." *Musicals 101*. Musicals 101, Ltd., 2006. Web. 1 June 2017. <https://www.musicals101.com/blackcrook.htm>.

Sokol, Samantha. "On This Day in NYC History, January 29th, 1798: The Park Theater Opened as the First Major Theater in NYC." *Untapped Cities*. Untapped Cities, Ltd., 29 Jan. 2014. Web. 1 June 2017. <http://untappedcities.com/2014/01/29/on-this-day-in-nyc-history-january-29th-the-park-theater-opened-as-the-first-major-theater-in-nyc/>.

Editors, MCNY. "John Street Theatre, the only show in town!" *MCNY Blog: New York Stories*. WordPress, 10 Jan. 2017. Web. 2 June 2017. <https://blog.mcny.org/2017/01/10/john-street-theatre-the-only-show-in-town/>.

Kenrick, John. "Demolished Broadway Theatres - Hi to L." *Musicals 101*. Musicals 101, Ltd., 2005. Web. 2 June 2017. <https://www.musicals101.com/bwaypast3b.htm#John>.

Editors, Revolvy. " Bowery Theatre ." *Revolvy*. Revolvy, LLC, 5 Apr. 2017. Web. 2 June 2017. <https://www.revolvy.com/topic/Bowery%20Theatre&item_type=topic>.

Editors, Rachel Friends. "Niblo's Garden." *Rachel Friends*. MediaWiki, 28 July 2015. Web. 2 June 2017. <http://rachelfriends.org:81/wikipedia_en_all_2016-02/A/Niblo%27s_Garden.html>.

Editors, Wired New York. "Niblo's Garden - Broadway & Prince St." *Wired New York*. VBulletin Solutions, Inc., 12 Sept. 2005. Web. 2 June 2017. <http://wirednewyork.com/forum/showthread.php?t=7266>.

Hernandez, Miguel. "The Astor Place Riot/Shakespeare Riots of 1849." *The New York History Blog*. Miguel Hernandez, 2 Jan. 2017. Web. 2 June 2017. <http://newyorkhistoryblog.org/2017/01/02/the-astor-place-riotshakespeare-riots-of-1849/>.

Editors, Revolvy. " Astor Opera House ." *Revolvy*. Revolvy, LLC, 14 Feb. 2017. Web. 2 June 2017. <https://www.revolvy.com/main/index.php?s=Astor%20Opera%20House>.

Doherty, Serena. "THIS IS HOW YOU BURLESQUE… LYDIA THOMPSON." *Burlexe*. Burlexe, Inc., 11 May 2016. Web. 2 June 2017. <http://www.burlexe.com/burlesque/lydia-

thompson-burlesque-victorian/>.

Editors, Burlesque & Cabaret. "Superstars of Burlesque: Lydia Thompson." *Burlesque & Cabaret*. Academy of Burlesque and Cabaret, Ltd., 11 Jan. 2015. Web. 2 June 2017. <http://www.burlesqueandcabaret.com/superstars-of-burlesque/lydia-thompson/>.

Editors, Encyclopedia Britannica. "Tony Pastor." *Encyclopedia Britannica*. Encyclopedia Britannica, Inc., 20 July 1998. Web. 2 June 2017. <https://www.britannica.com/biography/Tony-Pastor>.

Editors, Virtual Vaudeville. "What Is Vaudeville?" *Virtual Vaudeville*. University of Georgia Press, 2004. Web. 2 June 2017. <http://www.virtualvaudeville.com/hypermediaNotes/WhatIsVaudevilleF.html>.

Bradford, Wade. "Definition of Farce." *Thought Company*. Thought Company, Inc., 16 Apr. 2014. Web. 3 June 2017. <https://www.thoughtco.com/definition-of-farce-2713171>.

Editors, University of Virginia Library. "Blackface Minstrelsy." *University of Virginia Library*. University of Virginia Library, 2001. Web. 3 June 2017. <http://twain.lib.virginia.edu/huckfinn/minstrl.html>.

Editors, The British Players. "About Pantomime." *The British Players*. The British Players Organization, 2017. Web. 3 June 2017. <http://www.britishplayers.org/aboutpantomime.html>.

Editors, Brown University Library. "Broadway: The American Musical." *Brown University Library*. Brown University Library, 2005. Web. 3 June 2017. <http://library.brown.edu/exhibits/archive/broadway/trip.html>.

Simpson, Janice. "Pivotal Moments in Broadway's Black History." *Playbill*. Playbill, Inc., 22 Feb. 2015. Web. 3 June 2017. <http://www.playbill.com/article/pivotal-moments-in-broadways-black-history-com-342101>.

Padgett, Ken. "Blackface! Minstrel Shows." *Black-Face.Com*. Ken Padgett, 2011. Web. 3 June 2017. <http://black-face.com/minstrel-shows.htm>.

Lott, Eric. ""The Seeming Counterfeit": Racial Politics and Early Blackface Minstrelsy." *JStor*. The Johns Hopkins University Press, June 1991. Web. 3 June 2017. <https://www.jstor.org/stable/2712925?seq=1#page_scan_tab_contents>.

Andrews, Evan. "Was Jim Crow a real person?" *Ask History*. A&E Television Networks, LLC, 29 Jan. 2014. Web. 3 June 2017. <http://www.history.com/news/ask-history/was-jim-crow-a-real-person>.

Kenrick, John. "1700-1865: Musical Pioneers." *Musicals 101*. Musicals 101, Ltd., 2014. Web. 4 June 2017. <https://www.musicals101.com/1700bway.htm>.

Editors, Black Past. "African Company / African Grove Theatre." *Black Past*. Humanities Washington, 2017. Web. 4 June 2017. <http://www.blackpast.org/aah/african-company-african-grove-theatre>.

Verity, Michael. "What is Ragtime?" *Thought Company*. Thought Company, Inc., 25 June 2016. Web. 4 June 2017. <thoughtco.com/what-is-ragtime-2039546>.

Editors, Biography.Com. "Scott Joplin." *Biography.Com*. A&E Television Networks, LLC, 29 June 2015. Web. 4 June 2017. <https://www.biography.com/people/scott-joplin-9357953>.

Editors, Library of Congress. "History of Ragtime." *Library of Congress*. Library of Congress, 2017. Web. 4 June 2017. <https://www.loc.gov/item/ihas.200035811/>.

Mohr, Betty. "Opening the Vaults: Wonders of the 1893 World's Fair." *Le Bon Travel & Culture*. Le Bon Travel & Culture, LLC, 2015. Web. 4 June 2017. <http://lebontravel-culture.com/opening-the-vaults-wonders-of-the-1893-worlds-fair.html>.

Editors, College HipHop. "The Coon Song and How A Racist Chicago Cop Inspired Ragtime Music." *College HipHop*. WordPress, 17 Feb. 2015. Web. 4 June 2017. <http://collegehiphop.com/2015/02/17/ragtimemusic/>.

Editors, PBS. "Bert Williams." *Broadway: The American Musical Online*. Educational Broadcasting Corporation, 2015. Web. 4 June 2017. <http://www.pbs.org/wnet/broadway/stars/bert-williams/>.

Editors, New Amsterdam Theatre. " New Amsterdam Theatre History." *New Amsterdam Theatre*. New Amsterdam Theatre, 2015. Web. 4 June 2017. <http://www.newamsterdamtheatre.net/history.htm>.

Mroczka, Paul. "Olive Thomas: Broadway's New Amsterdam Ghost." *Broadway Scene*. Broadway Scene, Ltd., 2 Jan. 2014. Web. 4 June 2017. <http://broadwayscene.com/olive-thomas-broadways-new-amsterdam-ghost/>.

Editors, Daytonian in Manhattan. "The 1903 Art Nouveau "New Amsterdam" Theatre." *Daytonian in Manhattan*. Blogspot, 16 Sept. 2010. Web. 4 June 2017. <http://daytoninmanhattan.blogspot.tw/2010/09/1903-art-nouveau-new-amsterdam-theatre.html>.

Lebourdais, George Philip. "The Story of Art Nouveau." *Artsy.Net*. Artsy, LLC, 23 Nov. 2016. Web. 4 June 2017. <https://www.artsy.net/article/artsy-editorial-art-nouveau>.

Gude, Julian. "O.J. Gude and me." *Julians.Name: Renaissance Man in Training*. WordPress, 18 Dec. 2005. Web. 4 June 2017. <https://julians.name/2005/12/18/oj-gude-and-me/>.

Editors, History Channel. "New York City subway opens." *History Channel*. A&E Television Networks, LLC, 27 Oct. 2013. Web. 4 June 2017. <http://www.history.com/this-day-in-history/new-york-city-subway-opens>.

Editors, The Telegraph. "History of Times Square." *The Telegraph*. Telegraph Media Group, Ltd., 27 July 2011. Web. 4 June 2017. <http://www.telegraph.co.uk/news/worldnews/northamerica/usa/8664743/History-of-Times-Square.html>.

Holliday, Kathryn. "A TOWER TO "WAKE UP THE NATION"." *News Paper Spires*. The Skyscraper Museum, 2012. Web. 5 June 2017. <http://skyscraper.org/EXHIBITIONS/PAPER_SPIRES/nw13_tt.php>.

Dunlap, David W. "1907-8 | The Times Drops the Ball." *Times Insider*. The New York Times Company, 1 Jan. 2015. Web. 5 June 2017. <https://www.nytimes.com/times-insider/2015/01/01/1907-8-the-times-drops-the-ball/?_r=0>.

Trapnell, Kerri. "History of NYC Streets: The Great White Way." *Untapped Cities*. Untapped Cities, Ltd., 6 Dec. 2012. Web. 5 June 2017. <http://untappedcities.com/2012/12/06/history-of-streets-the-great-white-way/>.

Editors, Theater Seat Store. "The History of Broadway Theater." *Theater Seat Store*. Theater Seat Store, LLC, 2016. Web. 5 June 2017. <http://www.theaterseatstore.com/history-of-broadway>.

Mroczka, Paul. "Broadway History: Florenz Ziegfeld Makes His Mark." *Broadway Scene*. Broadway Scene, Ltd., 8 Apr. 2014. Web. 5 June 2017. <http://broadwayscene.com/broadway-history-florenz-ziegfeld-makes-his-mark/>.

Editors, Biography.Com. "Eugene O'Neill ." *Biography.Com*. A&E Television Networks, LLC, 2 Apr. 2014. Web. 5 June 2017. <https://www.biography.com/people/eugene-oneill-9428728>.

Churchwell, Sarah. "Eugene O'Neill, master of American theatre." *The Guardian*. Guardian News and Media, Ltd., 30 Mar. 2012. Web. 5 June 2017. <https://www.theguardian.com/stage/2012/mar/30/eugene-o-neill-master-american-theatre>.

Rusie, Robert. "The Great Depression." *Talkin' Broadway*. Talkin' Broadway, Inc., 2016. Web. 5 June 2017. <http://www.talkinbroadway.com/bway101/5.html>.

Editors, MapSites. "World War II." *MapSites*. MapSites, Ltd., 1999. Web. 5 June 2017.
<http://www.mapsites.net/gotham01/webpages/alisonhannah/broadww2.html>.

Editors, PBS. "Oklahoma!" *The American Musical Online*. Educational Broadcasting
Corporation, 2015. Web. 5 June 2017. <http://www.pbs.org/wnet/broadway/shows/oklahoma/>.

Editors, PBS. "Shubert Brothers." *The American Musical Online*. Educational Broadcasting
Corporation, 2016. Web. 5 June 2017. <http://www.pbs.org/wnet/broadway/stars/shubert-
brothers/>.

Editors, Tony Awards. "An award for Excellence." *Tony Awards*. IBM Corporation, 2017.
Web. 5 June 2017. <http://www.tonyawards.com/en_US/history/>.

Rothman, Lily. "This Is the Woman the Tony Awards Are Named After." *Time*. Time, Inc., 8
June 2015. Web. 5 June 2017. <http://time.com/3903886/ton-awards-antoinette-perry-
history/?p=3903886?xid=tcoshare>.

Editors, History Channel. "PROHIBITION." *History Channel*. A&E Television Networks,
LLC, 2016. Web. 5 June 2017. <http://www.history.com/topics/prohibition>.

Wirth, Jennifer. "Before Prohibition Ended, The 'Pansy Craze' Turned Big Cities Into One Big
Queer Party." *All Day*. All Day, Inc., 2016. Web. 5 June 2017. <http://www.allday.com/before-
prohibition-ended-the-pansy-craze-turned-big-cities-into-one-bi-2180825245.html>.

Blaney, Darren. "1964: The Birth of Gay Theater." *The Gay & Lesbian Review Worldwide*.
The Gay & Lesbian Review, LLC, 29 Dec. 2013. Web. 5 June 2017.
<http://www.glreview.org/article/1964-the-birth-of-gay-theater/>.

Keyes, Bob. "'Cats' was '80s most iconic musical, reinvigorated Broadway." *Press Herald*.
Maine Today Media, Inc., 28 Mar. 2013. Web. 5 June 2017.
<http://www.pressherald.com/2013/03/28/paws-in-the-action_2013-03-28/>.

Editors, The Phantom of the Opera. "FACTS & FIGURES." *The Phantom of the Opera
Official Website*. The Really Useful Group, 2016. Web. 5 June 2017.
<http://www.thephantomoftheopera.com/facts-figures/>.

Oswald, Anjelica. "'Hamilton' tickets sell for more than $2,000 — here's how much money
Broadway's hottest musical is raking in." *Business Insider*. Business Insider, Inc., 13 Apr. 2016.
Web. 5 June 2017. <http://www.businessinsider.com/hamilton-musical-revenue-facts-2016-
4/#the-broadway-run-has-earned-617-million-at-the-box-office-through-april-3-11>.

Pomerantz, Dorothy. "'Book Of Mormon' Brings In $19 Million Per Month." *Forbes*. Forbes,
Inc., 14 Jan. 2013. Web. 5 June 2017.

<https://www.forbes.com/sites/dorothypomerantz/2013/01/14/book-of-mormon-brings-in-19-million-per-month/#57a346c8614a>.

Peitzman, Louis. "Who Tells Their Story?" *Buzzfeed*. Buzzfeed, Inc., 29 Sept. 2016. Web. 5 June 2017. <https://www.buzzfeed.com/louispeitzman/asian-american-diversity-on-broadway?utm_term=.gg6KVa2JX#.fqpDbRNLQ>.

Editors, Asian American Theatre Revue. "Asian Actors and the Tonys...." *Asian American Theatre Revue Blog*. Asian American Theatre Revue, 9 May 2015. Web. 5 June 2017. <http://aatrevue.com/Newsblog/2015/05/09/asian-actors-and-the-tonys/>.

Van Winkle Keller, Kate. *Dance and Its Music in America, 1528-1789 (Ex)* . N.p.: Pendragon Press, 2007. Print.

Wilmeth, Don B. *The Cambridge History of American Theatre*. Vol. 3. N.p.: Cambridge U Press, 2006. Print. Cambridge History of American Theatre.

Slide, Anthony. *The Encyclopedia of Vaudeville*. N.p.: U Press of Mississippi, 2012. Print.

Robinson, Cedric J. *Forgeries of Memory and Meaning: Blacks and the Regimes of Race in American Theater and Film before World War II*. 1st ed. N.p.: The U of North Carolina Press, 2007. Print.

Peterson, Bernard L., Jr. *Early Black American Playwrights and Dramatic Writers: A Biographical Directory and Catalog of Plays, Films, and Broadcasting Scripts*. Annotated ed. N.p.: Greenwood, 1990. Print.

Free Books by Charles River Editors

We have brand new titles available for free most days of the week. To see which of our titles are currently free, click on this link.

Discounted Books by Charles River Editors

We have titles at a discount price of just 99 cents everyday. To see which of our titles are currently 99 cents, click on this link.

Made in United States
Orlando, FL
30 October 2022

24061887R00059